Windows NT 4

FOR BUSY PEOPLE

Windows NT 4

FOR BUSY PEOPLE

Stephen L. Nelson

Osborne/**McGraw-Hill**

Berkeley / New York / St. Louis / San Francisco / Auckland / Bogotá
Hamburg / London / Madrid / Mexico City / Milan / Montreal / New Delhi
Panama City / Paris / São Paulo / Singapore / Sydney / Tokyo / Toronto

Osborne/**McGraw-Hill**
2600 Tenth Street
Berkeley, California 94710
U.S.A.

For information on translations or book distributors outside the U.S.A., or to arrange bulk purchase discounts for sales promotions, premiums, or fundraisers, please contact Osborne/**McGraw-Hill** at the above address.

Windows NT 4 for Busy People

1234567890 DOC 99876

ISBN 0-07-882254-8

Publisher: Brandon A. Nordin
Acquisitions Editor: Joanne Cuthbertson
Project Editor: Mark Karmendy
Copy Editor: Kathryn Hashimoto
Proofreaders: Stefany Otis, Cynthia Douglas, Heidi Poulin
Indexer: Valerie Robbins
Computer Designers: Roberta Steele, Leslee Bassin, Peter F. Hancik
Quality Control: Joe Scuderi
Series and Cover Designer: Ted Mader Associates
Series Illustrator: Daniel Barbeau

To Elizabeth and Britt-Marie, who enrich my life in ways too numerous to list

About the Author

Stephen Nelson, a best-selling author and consultant, has written over 50 books and more than 100 articles on using computers for personal and business financial management. His books have sold over one million copies in English and have been translated into 11 different languages.

Contents at a glance

1   The Lay of the Land   1

2   Getting Started   15

3   Windows, Commands, and Dialog Boxes   31

4   Working with Documents and Disks   53

5   Printing   73

6   Using NT's Security   89

7   Handy NT Accessories   115

8   Power User Tools   135

9   Using the Internet with Windows NT   165

10 Customizing NT Workstations   177

11 Fine-Tuning NT   205

A   Installing Windows NT Workstation   219

B   Setting up a Small Windows NT Network   225

C   Emergency Search and Reserve   233

D   What's in Microsoft BackOffice   241

E   Table of MS-DOS and NT Commands   247

    Index   253

Contents

Acknowledgments, xv

Introduction, xvii

1 The Lay of the Land **1**

Fast Forward **2**

What's an Operating System? 3

What's So Special About the Windows NT Operating
System? 4

The Speed Thing 5

The Security Thing 6

The Safety Thing 8

The Wrong Reason—Maybe 9

There's Always a Catch— What Is It? 9

The Cost Factor 10

The Complexity Factor 10

The Hardware Compatibility Factor 11

On From Here 11

2 Getting Started **15**

Fast Forward **16**

Log On to NT 18

Start Programs 19

Using the Start Button 20

Using Shortcut Icons 21

Opening Documents to Start Programs 22

Run Multiple Programs 23

Stop Programs 24

Logging Off, Locking Up, and Shutting Down 25

Turning Off Your Computer 26

Logging Off So Someone Else Can Log On 27

Locking Your Computer 27

On From Here 28

3   Windows, Commands, and Dialog Boxes **31**

Fast Forward **32**

Windows, Windows Everywhere 34

Moving, Resizing, and Closing Windows 36

Working With Menus and Commands 38

Your First Menu Command 39

Working with Dialog Boxes 40

Using Toolbars 45

Using Shortcut Menus 46

Help! 47

On From Here 50

4   Working with Documents and Disks **53**

Fast Forward **54**

Using My Computer 56

Starting My Computer 57

Viewing a Disk's Contents 58

Doing Stuff with Files 60

Managing Your Disks 63

Formatting Floppy Disks 63

Monitoring Disk Space 64

Sharing Disks 66

Exploring Your Network 67

An Overview of Network Neighborhood 67

Mapping Network Drives 68

Working with Network Drives and Folders 70

On From Here 71

5   Printing **73**

Fast Forward **74**

Understanding How NT Prints 76

Installing Local and Network Printers 77

Adding a Local Printer 77

Adding a Network Printer 81

Printing a Document 82

Working With a Printer 83

Using the Document Commands 84

Using the Printer Commands 86

On From Here 86

6 Using NT's Security **89**

Fast Forward **90**

Understanding NT's Security 93

Accounts Work Like Country Club Memberships . . . 93

Rights Amount to Special Privileges 94

Permissions Control Access to Specific
Resources 95

Groups Simplify the Poor Administrator's
Workload 95

Audit Logs Monitor Your Work 95

Working With Accounts and Groups 96

Creating a New Account 97

Editing an Existing Account 98

Creating a New Group 98

Editing an Existing Group 99

Specifying Account Policies 100

Working With Rights 101

Working With Permissions 102

Setting Share Permissions on a FAT Disk 103

Setting Permissions on an NTFS Disk 106

Setting Permissions on a Printer 108

Working With Audit Logs 110

On From Here 112

7 Handy NT Accessories **115**

Fast Forward **116**

Using Calculator 118

Calculator Basics 118

Moving Values from and to the Calculator 121

Using the Scientific View of the Calculator 121

Using Paint 123

Painting Basics 123

Editing Images 126

Saving, Opening, and Printing Images 127

Using Phone Dialer 128

Using Wordpad 130

WordPad Basics 130

Editing WordPad Documents 131

Saving, Opening, and Printing WordPad
Documents 132

On From Here 133

8 Power User Tools **135**

Fast Forward **136**

Using Windows NT Explorer 139

NT Explorer Basics 139

Working with Files and Folders 141

Using the Ms-dos Command Prompt 149

Starting and Using the Command Prompt 149

Copying and Pasting Data to and from a Console
Window 151

Customizing the Console Window 152

Using Event Viewer 154

Starting and Using the Event Viewer 155

Using the Application Log 157

Using the Security Log 157

A Few More Comments About Event Viewer 159

More Power User Tools 161

Using the Back Up Program 161

Using Disk Administrator 162

Using Windows NT Diagnostics 162

On From Here 162

9 Using the Internet with Windows NT **165**

Fast Forward **166**

Connecting to the Internet With NT 167

Browsing the World Wide Web With Internet Explorer . . 169

Using Hyperlinks to Move Between Web Pages . . . 169

Paging to Previous or Next Web Page 171

Creating and Using Favorite Places 172

Saving Content 172

Forms Work Like Dialog Boxes 174

Closing Caveats and Comments 174

On From Here 174

10 Customizing NT Workstations **177**

Fast Forward **178**

Creating Shortcut Icons For Your Desktop 180

Creating Shortcuts on the Desktop 181

Deleting and Renaming Shortcut Icons 182

Arranging Shortcut Icons 182

Redecorating Your Desktop 183

Changing the Color Scheme 183

Changing Individual Elements of the Color
Scheme 185

Adjusting the Desktop Background 185

Customizing Your Menus 187

Customizing the Task Bar 187

Customizing the Start Menu 188

Clearing the Document Menu 190

Customizing NT Explorer and My Computer 190

Adjusting the View 191

Specifying the Level of File Information 193

Adding and Removing Programs 194

Adding a Program 194

Removing a Program 195

Changing Regional Settings 195

Adjusting Your System Date and Time 197

Changing the Keyboard and Mouse Settings 199

Adjusting Your Keyboard Keys 199

Adjusting the Way Your Mouse Works 200

Changing NT Sounds 201

On From Here 202

11   Fine-Tuning NT **205**

Fast Forward **206**

Using the Task Manager 208

Starting Task Manager 208

Managing Application Programs 209

Adjusting System Process Priorities 210

Reviewing Resource Usage 212

Using Nt's Disk Compression 213

Compressing a Disk 213

Uncompressing a Disk 214

Using the System Tool 215

On From Here 216

A   Installing Windows NT Workstation **219**

Getting Ready to Install Windows NT 220

Installing Windows NT Yourself 222

Getting Set up After You've Installed
Windows NT 223

B   Setting up a Small Windows NT Network **225**

Getting Ready 226

Installing Windows NT Server 228

Administering a Windows NT Network 229

Some Closing Comments 230

C   Emergency Search and Rescue **233**

Finding Missing Computers 234

Finding Lost Files and Folders 236

D   What's in Microsoft BackOffice **241**

The Bird's-Eye View 242

What's in BackOffice 243

E   Table of MS-DOS and NT Commands **247**

Index **253**

ACKNOWLEDGMENTS

A book like this is really a group project. Lots of people contribute in all sorts of ways. So I want to thank them here right up front.

Thank you, Joanne Cuthbertson, acquisitions editor for conceiving this book idea, organizing much of the material, and then (most of all) for letting me have the fun of writing it. Thank you, Heidi Poulin and Gordon Hurd, for playing the role of friendly traffic cops and thereby keeping contracts and chapters flying up and down the West Coast. Thank you, Mark Karmendy, project editor, Cynthia Douglas and Heidi Poulin (again), associate project editors, for getting this book together in such a short time. Thank you, Kathryn Hashimoto, copy editor, for a great job and pertinent suggestions. Last but not least, a special thank you to the folks in Osborne/McGraw-Hill's production department— Lance Ravella, Richard Whitaker, Leslee Bassin, Roberta Steele, Peter F. Hancik, and Joe Scuderi—you did a wonderful job at laying out the pages of this book.

Steve Nelson
July 23, 1996

INTRODUCTION

Every once in a while, a really exciting product comes along. A product that's not just a bunch of hype—that's not the result of some slick advertising or promotional campaign. At the risk of sounding daffy, I want to suggest to you that the newest version of Windows NT is just such a product. Windows NT (in combination with the cheap yet powerful hardware now available) provides people like you and me with tons of accessible, safe horsepower. Kind of like a hydroelectric plant. You can do *more*. You can do it *more safely*. And you can do it *more easily*.

Unfortunately—and this is just a minor annoyance, really—Windows NT requires a bit of learning on the part of its users. A little up-front investment. And that's what this book as well as all the others on the bookstore shelves are for.

Why this Book?

The basic premise of this book is simple. You're a busy guy. Or gal. And you don't want to and can't spend the time required to get the equivalent of a graduate degree in network operating systems. I hear you. And so does the publisher. This book gives you the lowdown on the Windows NT Workstation 4.0 in as expeditious a fashion as it possibly can. Restated in a slightly different way, I respect your time. I know you have other things to do with your life. So this book amounts to a fast-paced (but fun-paced) romp through the information you'll need to become proficient using Windows NT Workstation 4.0.

I have to tell you one other thing, too. (And I'm not just salving my own ego. Or at least I don't think so.) This book is fundamentally different from the other Windows NT books you see or saw on the bookstore shelves. This book doesn't just describe "how," it also explains "why." And this book doesn't bog you down with painfully detailed discussions of stuff you'll never need to know. The other books (and I read most of them as part of my research) don't do this. You'll read about all sorts of technically neat stuff, no doubt. But I figure you don't have time to get into a lengthy discussion of the pros and cons of all of the little nuances and subtleties of the networking protocols. I figure you're a big picture person.

How this Book Is Organized

Windows NT 4 for Busy People provides 11 chapters and five appendixes. You can take a look at the table of contents if you're curious about where I stuck stuff. But I do want to mention a handful of quick points about what the different chapters cover. For starters, you should definitely read or at least review the first two chapters. They introduce the big picture and explain how you start Windows NT and its programs. Even if you've spent the last year working with Windows 95 or the earlier version of Windows NT (version 3.51), you'll benefit by perusing these two chapters.

People experienced with a graphical user interface—say they've been using Windows 3.*x* or an Apple Macintosh—can skip Chapter 3, by the way. People who don't know what I mean by a graphical user interface (and are now scratching their heads wondering if they got the right book) should read Chapter 3.

I suggest that everyone read Chapter 4. It describes in detail how you work with disks, files, and the network. It should save you hours and hours of time. No kidding.

The rest of the chapters cover a hodgepodge of topics. You can refer to the table of contents for specifics, but let me say that new users will probably benefit most from Chapter 5 (it covers printing) and Chapter 7 (it describes a handful of the freebie programs that come with Windows NT). Experienced users will probably benefit most from Chapter 6 (it covers NT's security features), from Chapter 8 (it and discusses NT's power user tools), from Chapter 10 (it describes how you customize Windows NT) and from Chapter 11 (it explains how you performance-tune Windows NT). Anybody who's interested in the Internet—and more specifically in the World Wide Web—should con-sider reviewing Chapter 9 (it describes NT's Internet Jumpstart Kit).

I also included a few appendixes. Appendix A explains how you install Windows NT Workstation. Or, actually that's not quite right. What Appendix A really does is try to convince you to pay someone else to install the software. (Appendix A does give you the information you need to give this person appropriate directions.) On a whim, I included Appendix B. It explains (in general terms) how you set up a small Windows NT network. Autobiographical in nature, Appendix B attempts to convince you that if you're a business owner or manage some small organization, you can and should set up and administer your own small NT network. Appendix C acts as an emergency reference for finding lost files, something everyone needs to do every once in a while. Appendix D is a discussion of Microsoft's BackOffice, a group of software products that Microsoft sells for NT client-server networks. And finally comes Appendix E, which is a table of MS-DOS and NT commands.

Conventions Used Here

Busy People books use several common conventions. So that you get maximum value from your reading, let me explain them quickly.

FAST FORWARD

Each regular chapter begins with a FAST FORWARD that summarizes the main points of the chapter. You can use a FAST FORWARD to preview the chapter's material. If you've already read the chapter or you know the material covered in the chapter, you can also use the FAST FORWARD to review the chapter's information. (For example, if you were back in college and you were studying for a test, you could probably use the FAST FORWARDs as a study review.)

habits & strategies

You'll find that habits & strategies marginalia pepper the pages of this book. These amount to little tangential asides where I clue you in to some trick you may want to try or some technique you want to know about.

Margin Note

Every so often there's a miscellaneous bit of information that doesn't quite fit into the normal flow of the chapter—but that's still useful. I stuck these blurbs into the margins as notes.

CAUTION

You can't get into too much trouble using Windows NT. Safety should be its middle name. Even so, there are a few places where you'll want to be careful. To make these warnings stand out, I placed them into the margin as CAUTIONs.

SHORTCUT

Oops. Almost forgot. I also scattered some quick-and-dirty shortcut ideas around. You'll see these set off as a margin elements identified as SHORTCUTs.

definition

Usually, I explain computer or networking jargon in the text, wherever the technobubble first occurs. But if you encounter words you don't recognize, look for this body builder in the margin. Definitions point out important terms you reasonably might not know the meaning of. When necessary they're strict and a little technical, but most of the time they're informal and conversational.

ON FROM HERE

As mentioned earlier, the place to start is Chapter 1. After that, you'll want to proceed to Chapter 2. And after that, well, pick your pleasure.

The Lay of the Land

INCLUDES

- What is an operating system?

- What's so special about the Windows NT operating system?

- What problems does the Windows NT operating system present?

FAST FORWARD

UNDERSTAND OPERATING SYSTEMS ➤ *pp. 3-4*

An operating system manages the physical components—the gadgetry—of your computer. A network operating system like Windows NT also manages connections to other computers. NT employs a server computing model, arranging networks of computers into client workstations and servers.

REVIEW WINDOWS NT'S ADVANTAGES ➤ *pp. 4-9*

Windows NT provides three principal advantages. As a true 32-bit operating system that supports symmetric processing, it's fast. It provides sophisticated built-in security to control access to the workstation and access to specific files, folders, and disks. Finally, it uses separate address spaces to prevent one errant program from crashing other programs.

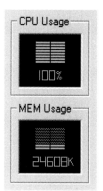

REVIEW WINDOWS NT'S DISADVANTAGES ➤ *pp. 9-11*

Windows NT presents three problems to its users, too. Windows NT costs more than other PC desktop operating systems (such as Windows 95) to purchase, install, and support. Windows NT represents a quantum leap in complexity. Finally, Windows NT works on a rather limited set of computers and equipment (at least compared to MS-DOS or Windows 95).

I particularly like this one travel writer. One of the neat things he does is give the lay of the land at the start of each of his books. If you get his book on visiting England, for example, he tells you a bit about the country, its history, and Queen Elizabeth. I want to do the same thing here. Windows NT Workstation, the subject of this book, really does resemble a different country in many ways—especially for those people who are used to desktop operating systems like MS-DOS, Apple Macintosh's MacOS, or the other Microsoft Windows products. So almost everybody will benefit by getting some background information on what's so neat about this product—and about why you'll occasionally want to pull your hair out.

To organize this discussion, I'm going to ask and answer three questions about NT (as I'll call it in the pages of this book). That way, you can easily find the answers to questions you may have.

WHAT'S AN OPERATING SYSTEM?

I've already used a phrase—operating system—that some people aren't going to be all that comfortable with. So let me explain. An *operating system* just manages the physical components—the gadgetry—of your computer. Its storage disks. The monitor, memory, and your mouse. In short, everything that's screwed into or plugged into that box that you think of as your computer.

You could have individual application programs, such as a word processor or an accounting program, manage this stuff, but that approach would be really redundant. It would mean that every application program (I'll just start calling these programs) would have to include the same chunk of software instructions for saving some file of information to your hard disk or for printing some document. In comparison, by having the operating system handle this, individual programs can simply have the operating system do the work of messing around with the hardware. Your word processor can just say to the operating system, for example, "Oh, save this file to disk." And then the operating system can do all the work—finding empty space on the disk, placing the file in the space, and then keeping track of where the file is stored for when you later want to retrieve the file.

One interesting feature of Windows NT is that it's really a network operating system. In addition to knowing how to deal with all the gadgetry connected to your computer, NT also knows how to connect to other computers and get them to do stuff with their gadgetry. For example, if your computer and Fred's computer are connected together in the right way—in other words, if the two computers are *networked*— the version of NT that's running on your desktop computer can get Fred's computer to perform tasks like save files to its disk and print documents.

In fact, NT's networking is rather sophisticated. NT employs what's called a server computing model. This isn't the book to go into some long-winded discussion of client-server computing, but, in a nutshell, client-server computing arranges networks of computers into client workstations (which people like you and I use at our desks) and servers, which the network uses to handle the dirty work of computing: maintaining painfully detailed customer databases, for one example, and printing monstrously long reports for those yahoos in accounting, for another.

There are actually two flavors of Windows NT: Windows NT Workstation, which runs on client workstations, and Windows NT Server, which runs on servers. This book describes and focuses on the workstation version of NT.

WHAT'S SO SPECIAL ABOUT THE WINDOWS NT OPERATING SYSTEM?

This question really cuts to the heart of the matter. If you're working with computers already, you're probably already familiar with other operating systems such as MS-DOS or the other versions of Microsoft Windows or the Mac's operating system. Those operating systems work pretty well. So why all the hoopla (at least in some quarters) about NT? Why are you sitting here reading this book?

Fortunately, this question is pretty easy to answer. There are three good reasons people in the know select NT: speed, safety, and security. There's also one bad reason, which we'll also talk about.

The Speed Thing

NT's speed boils down to two features: NT is a true 32-bit operating system, and NT supports symmetric processing. Let's start with the 32-bit business. All that 32-bit means is that NT moves the 1's and 0's that computers understand in 32-digit, or 32-bit, chunks. This, for example, is a 32-bit chunk:

```
00101101001111010011001111010001
```

In comparison, MS-DOS and the earlier versions of Windows move their bits around in 16-bit chunks. This is a 16-bit chunk:

```
0101110100111001
```

You can see the difference, right? NT moves twice as much data at a time.

One writer suggested the following image: think about your microprocessor (the brains of a PC) as a bus with 32 seats. (I don't remember who the writer is or I would give him or her credit for a great analogy.) When MS-DOS or Windows 3.*x* drives the bus, it only lets 16 people ride at a time. So 16 seats are always empty. In comparison, when NT drives the bus, it lets 32 people ride at a time. The bus is always full. While it's true that the bus—to continue our simile—doesn't actually move any faster across town, it does get its work done twice as fast because it's carrying twice as many people. Moving 32 people from the airport to the hotel with NT, for example, requires a single trip. But moving 32 people from the airport to the hotel with, say, MS-DOS, requires two trips.

I should mention that a few parts of Windows 3.11 (a cousin to NT) move stuff around in 32-bit chunks. The much-ballyhooed Windows 95 moves stuff around in 32-bit chunks most (but not all) of the time.

So do OS/2 (IBM's desktop operating system) and MacOS (the Apple Mac's desktop operating system). And NT's real competitors—basically UNIX workstation operating systems—move stuff around in 32-bit chunks, too. So, to be quite honest, this "it's a 32-bit operating system" refrain isn't unique to NT. But for the 150 million people who spend some portion of their day sitting in front of a PC running MS-DOS and early versions of Windows 3.x, the 32-bit capability is unique. And it is cool.

Another feature of Windows NT is that it supports symmetric processing. *Symmetric processing* means that NT works on computers with more than one microprocessor. NT Workstation (which is what this book is about) works on computers with two microprocessors. NT Server will probably work on computers with up to 32 microprocessors. I say probably because I'm working with a beta version of the software to write this book, and the beta version of NT Server only supports four processors. The previous version of NT, however, supported up to 32 microprocessors. So I'm assuming that when the dust settles, the new version of NT Server will also support 32 microprocessors.

Normal folk like you and I don't really need a machine with dual microprocessors. But someone who works with a monstrously power-ful program that does all sorts of tricky calculations (like a CAD program, say) can get a nice performance boost from a multimicroprocessor computer. (To be fair, I need to note that this symmetric processing angle is a speed advantage only compared to earlier PC operating systems. The really popular UNIX operating systems support symmetric processing, too.)

The Security Thing

A second reason for NT's specialness is its built-in security. Security may sound like something only the clinically paranoid should worry about, but I want to suggest that this perspective stems from our complacency about computer security issues. Let me explain.

The problem with any of the desktop operating systems—MS-DOS, any of the other versions of Microsoft Windows, OS/2, and the MacOS—is that the operating system really can't control who has access to and who can modify a file stored on the computer's hard disk.

That sounds esoteric, I know. But it actually presents a rather serious set of problems as soon as you start networking computers or start sharing computers among a bunch of different people.

Take, for example, the simple case of my little business. We're really small. Depending on the time of the year, we have maybe three or four employees. Maybe two or three subcontractors regularly visit us in our offices or have access to our little network. With an operating system that doesn't worry about security, anybody who knows how to boot a computer using MS-DOS can gain access to all the information stored on that computer. In other words, they can boot one of our PCs using MS-DOS and then start reading, writing, updating, and deleting files. (Just so you know, to *boot* a computer with MS-DOS, you stick in a floppy disk that's been formatted as a "system disk" into your A drive and then restart the machine.)

"Now wait a minute," you're thinking, "that can't happen with our system. The accounting software requires a password before someone can gain entry." Unfortunately, that's not quite right. Recall what I said earlier about operating systems: it's really the operating system that does all the work of fiddling with your files on disk. A program can prevent someone from gaining access to a file via that program. But it can't prevent someone from gaining access directly from the operating system or from gaining access using some other program (such as one that doesn't require a password). As a result, some miscreant with evil on his mind can go in and fiddle with or view highly confidential information: last year's profits, next year's salaries, or correspondence with your attorney. Somebody else as dumb as a box of rocks can delete or corrupt files. Your technically astute teenager can even inadvertently introduce a computer virus.

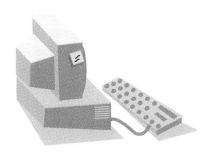

With NT, however, none of this has to happen for a couple of reasons. First, NT won't let someone else use a computer unless the person trying to use the computer supplies his or her name and a valid password. So only people you know can use your computer. Second, NT doesn't let a user (the person who supplied his or her name and password) access a file unless he or she is on the list of people who can fool around with the file. I'll talk more about security in Chapter 6.

The Safety Thing

Let me quickly mention one other important aspect of NT: its safety. The safety thing is a little tricky, technically. But as long as we keep our discussion really general, neither of us will get too confused. Here's the deal: on a computer running MS-DOS (which includes any computer running the older versions of Windows that came before Windows 95 and Windows NT), when one program freaks out, it might cause the other programs that were running to also go toes up. Suppose, for example, you're working on your word processor, writing the sales proposal of your life. And for fun, let's also say you've got some other program running too—maybe a presentation program. If the presentation program freaks out (and *crashes*), your word processor may also crash. And in the process, you'll probably lose your sales proposal. Your working environment, then, is only as safe as your most unstable program. Or, to use a cliché, the chain is only as strong as its weakest link.

NT, however, changes all of this. It basically acts like an overzealous playground monitor. If NT sees some program attempting to get crazy, NT prevents the program from doing any damage to other programs or their data. The errant program may corrupt its own data, of course. But at least it won't also corrupt other programs' data. (In a nutshell, what NT does is make each program play in its own separate area of memory.)

I don't want to editorialize too much here. But I want to emphasize that the safety angle is important. Really important. Those of us who've been weaned on what some people have called hair ball operating systems (like MS-DOS and early versions of Microsoft Windows) have gotten used to living dangerously. Metaphorically speaking, we've not only been riding motorcycles, we've chosen to forego the protection of a helmet.

This cavalier, happy-go-lucky approach may work reasonably well when all you've been doing is working on your own little projects: a report, a business forecast, or some presentation. But it doesn't really cut the mustard when you're talking about mission-critical applications of a computer (like accounting) or really large-scale projects involving dozens or even hundreds of people (like an engineering R & D project).

Windows 95 provides some of the same playground-monitoring as does NT. Windows 95, however, isn't quite as sophisticated as NT. With Windows 95, an errant 16-bit Windows application can bring down other 16-bit Windows applications (16-bit Windows applications are those created especially for versions of Windows 3.x).

The Wrong Reason—Maybe

Honesty compels me to note that there's a fourth reason for NT's specialness. Or maybe that's not quite accurate. I should really say that there's a fourth reason—in addition to the speed, security, and safety reasons mentioned earlier—for NT's popularity: Microsoft Corporation produces the NT operating system.

Because Microsoft makes and sells NT, NT amounts to a pretty safe bet for companies making big investments in their computer systems. You've probably heard the line, often uttered by corporate systems managers and IBM salesmen, that "people don't get fired for buying IBM." The same thing can be said of NT and Microsoft Corporation. NT represents a safe bet. Choosing NT means you're buying a product from a big, dominant, well-positioned software company. NT may not be the best choice in every situation (you might do better with a UNIX operating system, for example), but it won't ever be the worst choice.

While this reasoning makes some people nauseous, it actually doesn't bother me. But I'm not a technology junkie; I'm really a business guy (if I still had any business suits that fit, I'd be known as a "suit" in some companies). So I don't feel uncomfortable with the notion of playing it safe in one area of your business so you can take your risks in other areas that you understand better or in other areas that offer bigger potential rewards. Running or managing a business presents enough risk as it is.

THERE'S ALWAYS A CATCH— WHAT IS IT?

I've always felt betrayed by writers who tout some product, service, or idea and then don't honestly alert you to the disadvantages and problems of what they're evangelizing. So before you and I wrap up this discussion, let's talk about what isn't right with NT—at least from the regular guy's or gal's perspective. There are, to be quite blunt, three current problems with NT: its cost, its complexity, and its limited hardware compatibility list. At least briefly, we should touch on all three points.

The Cost Factor

Without question, NT costs more than other PC desktop operating systems such as Windows 95. For starters, it's more expensive out of the box. An NT workstation license, for example, costs roughly twice what Windows 95 does. But that's the least of it.

My guess is that to run NT you'll want to have in the neighborhood of 32 megabytes of memory. (To run Windows 95, you want to have 16 megabytes or so.) At current prices, that extra 16 megabytes means that you're looking at about an extra $300 per computer. Add to that the extra $300 or so you'll spend for NT and the installation, and you're looking at almost an extra $600 per computer. That's not as much as a new computer, I guess. But if you've got, say, ten computers to upgrade or 100 computers to upgrade—well, you can do the math as well as I can.

I should also mention that NT costs more to support. Microsoft provides lots of different support options for NT. And reportedly Microsoft will help retail customers of NT Workstation get the operating system installed and working right for free. But after the first technical support call, you pay right around $200 per technical support call (if you call and try to sneak in two questions, they really will charge you twice, too!).

The Complexity Factor

My mother is sort of a PC nut. I don't know why, but she is. Anyway, she and Dad were always pretty thrifty with their money, and so they now find themselves in retirement with more than they need. An extra $600 wouldn't be that big a deal for them in the grand scheme of things. Even so, I would strongly discourage them from acquiring NT Workstation for their home PC. NT represents a quantum leap in complexity. It does some neat tricks, as you now know. But its 32-bit-ness, its security features, and its safety don't warrant its extra complexity for many users such as home users (like Mom and Dad), one-person businesses, and students.

The desktop operating systems like Apple Macintosh's MacOS and Microsoft's Windows 95 don't do as much as NT, but these other operating systems are much easier to use and are much easier to maintain.

Let me also make one tangential observation. If you've heard that Windows 95 and Windows NT use the same graphical user interface (which is true) and so they work the same way, let me clear up that misconception. Superficially, NT and Windows 95 look very much alike. But as soon as you dig deeper—as soon as you peel back a layer or two of the onion—you will find that they work and look very differently.

The Hardware Compatibility Factor

There's one final fly in the NT ointment. NT works on a very limited set of computers and equipment (at least compared to MS-DOS or Windows 95). For this reason, it's very likely you will have trouble getting NT to work just right unless you've purchased a computer that's made to run NT. This sounds incredible, I know. But it's really true.

I don't think this should make you throw up your hands and quit—at least not if NT's speed, security, and safety appeal to you. But the hardware compatibility factor probably does mean that you will need to get help getting NT to work correctly. NT will require some driver you're missing to use your sound card (this happened with my laptop). Or NT won't work with your CD drive because of reliability issues (this happened with my NT server). Or NT won't recognize your graphics card, so you'll have to fiddle around to get it working correctly (this happened with my desktop).

Ideally—and this is what I do now—you should purchase PCs that come with NT already installed. That way, you'll know everything works correctly. When you can't go this route because, let's say, you're upgrading existing computers, I strongly recommend that you pay someone else (such as the computer manufacturer or a systems consultant) to perform the actual installation work. Unless you're technically proficient and you're not all that busy, you'll find that installing NT requires more work than you can reasonably afford.

ON FROM HERE

You're ready to begin actually working with NT. So, when you've got the time, turn on your computer, and turn to Chapter 2. It describes how you start and stop NT and how you start and stop the programs you'll use. If you're new to graphical user interfaces like the one that

Driver: Basically, a special program that NT needs to communicate with a particular piece of gadgetry. For example, NT needs a printer driver to use your printer.

NT uses (say you've never used a Windows-based PC or an Apple Macintosh before), you'll also want to take a peek at Chapter 3. It describes how to work with windows and dialog boxes and how to choose menu commands and toolbar tools.

Getting Started

INCLUDES

- Starting NT and logging on

- Starting programs

- Running multiple programs at the same time

- Stopping programs

- Logging off, locking up, and shutting down

15

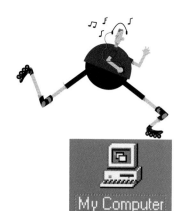

FAST FORWARD

LOG ON TO NT ➤ *pp. 18-19*

Turn on your computer to start NT. Wait until NT displays the Begin Logon message box. Press CTRL-ALT-DEL, then supply your user name and password. If necessary, select the correct domain from the Domain drop-down list box.

START PROGRAMS ➤ *pp. 19-23*

You typically start a program in one of three ways: using the Start button, using a shortcut icon, and by opening a document. To use the Start button, click the button and choose a program from the Start menu, the Programs menu, or one of the Programs menu's submenus. To use a desktop shortcut icon, just double-click the icon. (To double-click an object, you just point to it with the mouse and quickly click the mouse's left button twice.) To start a program by opening a document, indicate which document you want to open—such as by selecting it from the Documents menu.

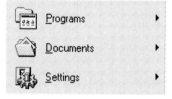

RUN MULTIPLE PROGRAMS ➤ *pp. 23-24*

NT possesses enough smarts and raw power to run multiple programs at a time. To run multiple programs, you simply start more than one. To switch between running programs, click the programs' buttons on the task bar. Clicking a program's task bar button moves that program to the foreground.

SHUT DOWN YOUR COMPUTER ➤ *pp. 25-26*

Click the Start button and choose the Shut Down command button. When NT displays the Shut Down Windows dialog box, choose the Shut down the computer? option button and then click Yes.

C Close all programs and log on as a different user?

LOG OFF YOUR COMPUTER ➤ *p. 27*

Click the Start button, select Shut Down, and then choose the Close all programs and log on as a different user? option button. When you click Yes, NT stops any of the programs you've started and then displays the logon message so someone else can log on.

Lock Workstation

LOCK YOUR COMPUTER ➤ *p. 27*

Press CTRL-ALT-DEL. When NT displays the Windows NT Security dialog box, click the Lock Workstation command button. To unlock your computer, press CTRL-ALT-DEL again, and then supply your user name and password.

Getting NT started—and starting the programs you'll use—isn't difficult. But if you're accustomed to a simpler desktop operating system, you'll need to learn how things work in NT. And that's what we'll do here.

I'll also explain how you run multiple programs—or *multitask*—from within NT. Normally, books like this stick multitasking information near the back of the book in a section entitled "Really Technical Stuff." But a discussion of NT's multitasking actually fits very nicely with a discussion about how you start NT and its programs. So we'll throw convention to the wind.

LOG ON TO NT

Starting NT doesn't really require any special effort on your part. You simply turn your computer on. Your computer then performs its power-on self-test, or POST. Then it loads the BIOS (which are really just a set of instructions required to jump-start your computer). And then NT displays the OS Loader menu, which asks you to choose an operating system. By default, the OS Loader picks NT if you don't select your other choice, the operating system you used before NT (probably MS-DOS or Windows 95). Then, after all of this, NT begins the rather slow and somewhat tedious process of loading itself. The key thing for you to note is that really, when you boil all of this information down to its very essence, all you have to do is turn on the computer. That's it. NT starts itself.

Once NT starts, however, you do need to log on, or sign on, to NT before you can begin using the computer. To do this, you wait until NT displays the Begin Logon message box. As the Begin Logon message indicates, you press CTRL-ALT-DEL to log on (press these three keys simultaneously). Next, NT displays the Logon Information dialog box.

You log on to identify yourself to NT, as a way of saying "Hey, NT? This is Steve and I want to start using some programs." To do this, you supply your user name (if the correct user name isn't already displayed) using the User Name box, you type your password into the Password box, and if necessary, you select the correct domain from the

CAUTION

If you're concerned about security, you should be careful when logging on. Someone can learn your password by observing which keys you type.

Domain drop-down list box. Then you click OK. If you don't know your user name, password, or domain, ask the network administrator (the person who set up your computer or installed NT for you).

Don't worry that the Logon Information dialog box displays asterisks in place of characters when you type your password. NT displays asterisks so somebody can't look over your shoulder and learn your password.

After you log on, NT displays the Windows NT desktop, as shown in Figure 2.1.

START PROGRAMS

After you start NT and log on to identify yourself, you're ready to start programs. There are about a dozen ways to start programs using NT, but three methods tend to be most useful: using the Start button, using a shortcut icon, and by opening a document. I describe all three methods here.

Figure 2.1 The Windows NT desktop appears after you successfully log on to Windows NT

Submenu: A subsequent menu

that appears when you choose

an item from a menu. An arrow-

head to the right of the menu

item indicates that a submenu is

available for that item.

Using the Start Button

The Start button is so easy to use that I'm almost embarrassed to mention it. Click the button labeled as Start (shown in the lower-left corner of the screen in Figure 2.1). You do this by moving the mouse so its pointer rests on the Start button and then clicking the mouse's left button. When you do, NT displays the Start menu (see Figure 2.2).

To continue, click on the Programs option. This tells NT to display a list of programs you've installed (or that someone else has installed) on your computer. To start a particular program, just click it.

A program can appear on any of the Start button's menus or submenus, which can be somewhat confusing. It all depends on how the person installing the program set it up. For example, sometimes programs appear on the Start menu itself. Sometimes a program appears on the Programs menu. And sometimes a program appears on a submenu of the Programs menu. Take a look at Figure 2.3 for an example. I selected the Accessories item on the Programs menu. That caused NT to display the Accessories submenu, which lists a bunch of additional programs and one other submenu called Multimedia.

You get the picture, right? You click the Start button to display the Start menu. Then, usually, you choose the Programs menu. Then you choose an item (a program), or sometimes you choose a submenu (like Accessories) and choose an item from it. Just to make sure that you know how this whole thing works, click the Start button, click Programs, click Accessories, and then click Calculator. This starts the NT Calculator

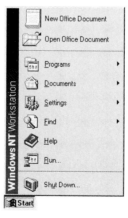

Figure 2.2 When you click the Start button, NT displays the Start menu

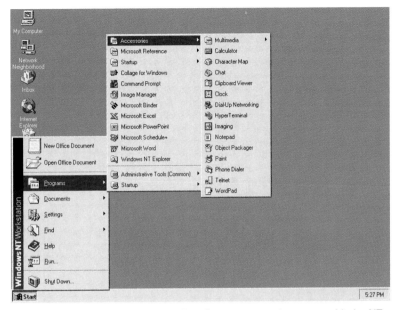

Figure 2.3 The Accessories menu lists free programs that come with the NT operating system

accessory, which works like a handheld calculator that you can use for quick computations.

You use the calculator in the same way that you use a handheld calculator, except that instead of pressing the calculator keys with your fingers, you click the mouse.

Using Shortcut Icons

Shortcut icons represent another way to start programs. If you take another look at the Windows NT desktop shown in Figure 2.1, you'll notice little pictures that appear along the left edge of the screen:

My Computer, Network Neighborhood, Inbox, Internet Explorer, Recycle Bin, and My Briefcase. These pictures, called *shortcut icons,* amount to clickable buttons you can use to quickly start the programs they represent. To use a shortcut icon, you just double-click it. For example, to start the Internet Explorer program, you just double-click its shortcut icon.

I'll talk more about shortcut icons in future chapters. In Chapter 4, for example, I'll explain how to start and use both the My Computer program and the Network Neighborhood program. In Chapter 10, I'll describe how you can create your own shortcut icons.

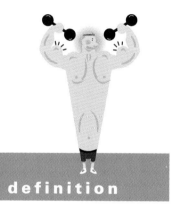

definition

Document: A file you've created using a program: a letter you've written using your word processor, a worksheet you've created with your spreadsheet program, or a picture you've created with a drawing program.

Opening Documents to Start Programs

NT is generally smart enough to know which program you use to fool around with a particular document. It can look at a word processing document, for example, and know that you need to start your word processor in order to use the document; similarly, it can look at a spreadsheet document and know that you need to start your spreadsheet program in order to use the document.

Because NT is this smart, you don't actually need to tell it to start a program. Instead, you can tell it to open a document. NT can then start the appropriate program and tell the program to "grab" the document.

You can open documents in a couple of ways: using the Document menu or using either My Computer's list or Windows NT Explorer's list of documents. You'll probably find the Documents menu is easiest to use. On the Documents menu, NT lists the last 15 documents you've worked with. The Documents menu item appears as an item on the Start menu (take another look at Figure 2.2 if you need to refresh your memory). So, one easy way to open any file that you've worked with recently is to select the file from the Documents menu. NT starts the appropriate program and directs it to open the file.

As mentioned earlier, you can also identify a document you want to work with by using the My Computer program or the Windows NT Explorer program. Chapter 4 explains in detail how you do this, but basically you start these programs by double-clicking the My Computer shortcut icon or by choosing Windows NT Explorer from the Programs menu. Then you use the My Computer or Windows NT Explorer program to display a list of the documents, or files, you've stored on your computer. When you see one you want to open, you just double-click it.

RUN MULTIPLE PROGRAMS

NT possesses enough smarts and raw power to run multiple programs at a time, or *multitask*. It's typical, for example, to run your word processor, an accessory or two (such as the Calculator program introduced earlier), and maybe even another big program such as a spreadsheet program.

While running multiple programs at the same time may seem silly or unnecessarily confusing, it's actually a really slick way to improve your productivity. You could, for example, download some large file from the Internet or an electronic bulletin board and at the same time use your word processor to write a report. Or you might want to use two programs concurrently—such as a spreadsheet program and a presentation program—to create a sales presentation for your best customer.

To run multiple programs, you simply start more than one. That's it.

When you run multiple programs, one of your programs is called the foreground process (a *process* is just a program you've started). This means it's the one whose window you'll see in front of all the program windows. And it's the one to which you'll issue commands.

NT places a button on the task bar for each program you start. To move a different program to the foreground, you simply click its task bar button. Figure 2.4 shows how the screen looks after I start the Calculator program and the WordPad program. Notice that the task bar, which appears along the bottom edge of the screen, shows the Calculator button and the WordPad button next to the Start button. Notice

CAUTION

How many programs you can successfully run depends largely on the amount of memory your computer has. With more memory, you can run more programs.

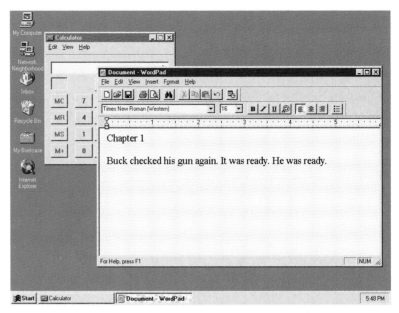

Figure 2.4 This Windows NT desktop shows two programs: Calculator running in the background, and WordPad running in the foreground

too that the WordPad window obscures the Calculator window. That's because the WordPad program is the foreground process.

Just to make sure you understand how running multiple programs, or multitasking, works, let's try it right now. Start the Calculator program first, then start the WordPad program (both the Calculator and WordPad programs appear on the Accessories submenu). Then click their task bar buttons to flip-flop between the two programs. Pretty easy, right?

STOP PROGRAMS

You typically stop programs either by issuing a command or by closing the program's window. I'm going to briefly describe both techniques here. But if you still have questions about the mechanics of either operation, take the time to peruse Chapter 3. It goes into much more detail about the ways you work with windows and choose commands.

The easiest way to stop a program is to click its Close button with the mouse. The Close button is the button whose face shows an X, and it appears in the upper-right corner of every program's window. If you earlier followed my suggestion to start the Calculator program, you'll need to stop it by clicking its Close button.

 —— Close button

You can also issue a command to a program to tell it to stop. How this works depends on the program. But, typically, the command at the bottom of the first (or left-most) menu is named something like Exit. You can choose this command by clicking on the menu name and then the menu option. To stop the WordPad program, for example, you click on the File menu and then click on the Exit command:

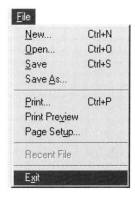

Don't, by the way, worry about the mechanics of clicking Close buttons and choosing menu commands here. In Chapter 3, I'll go into detail about all the ins and outs of working with NT's windows, commands, and dialog boxes.

LOGGING OFF, LOCKING UP, AND SHUTTING DOWN

Based on your identity—which NT establishes when you log on—NT lets you do certain activities (such as read, review, and change the files you've created). And it doesn't let you do certain other activities

When you close a program window, you sometimes need to save any information you've entered into the window before closing it. But we'll talk more about this in Chapter 3.

(such as read, review, and change the files of other network users). For these reasons, you don't want to leave your computer on, NT running, and your account still logged on when you go to lunch or head home for the night. If you do, someone else can completely circumvent the NT security system simply by sitting down in front of your computer and then continuing your session.

How you discontinue your Logon session, however, depends on how quickly you'll return to your computer and whether you want to turn it off while you're gone.

Turning Off Your Computer

If you want to turn off your computer—say because it's Friday afternoon and you're leaving for the weekend—click the Start button and choose the Shut Down command. Then, when NT displays the Shut Down Windows dialog box (shown in Figure 2.5), make sure the Shut down the computer? option button is selected (a dot appears inside the option button) and then click Yes. NT logs you off and then shuts down the operating system, saving any necessary information to disk. When NT finishes shutting down, it displays the onscreen message "It is now safe to turn off your computer."

If you want to restart the computer— which means you want to shut down NT and then have it restart itself, select the Restart the computer? option in the Shut Down Windows dialog box and then click Yes.

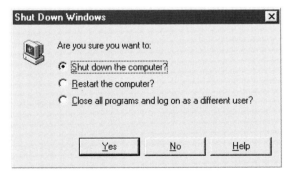

Figure 2.5 You can use the Shut Down Windows dialog box to end your logon session

Logging Off So Someone Else Can Log On

If you just want to log off so someone else can log on, click the Start button and choose the Shut Down command. Then, when NT displays the Shut Down Windows dialog box (see Figure 2.5), choose the Close all programs and log on as a different user? option button. NT stops any of the programs you've started and then displays the logon message "Press CTRL-ALT-DEL to log on." You or another user can then press CTRL-ALT-DEL to log on.

Locking Your Computer

If you want to stay logged on but don't want somebody else fooling around with your computer while you're gone—say you're taking a lunch break, for example—press CTRL-ALT-DEL. When NT displays the Windows NT Security dialog box (see Figure 2.6), click the Lock Workstation command button. To do this, move the mouse pointer so it rests on the Lock Workstation button and then click the mouse's left button. To later unlock the workstation, you'll need to press CTRL-ALT-DEL again and then, when prompted, provide NT with your user name and password.

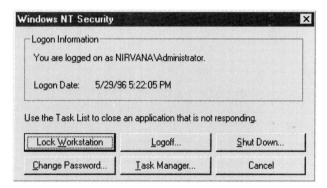

Figure 2.6 The Windows NT Security dialog box lets you lock your workstation

ON FROM HERE

You know how to start NT and how to start programs using NT. If you're comfortable working with a graphical user interface like the one that NT provides, you'll probably want to skip the next chapter (it's intended primarily for people who are new to graphical user interfaces). You probably will benefit, however, by taking a peek at the material covered in Chapters 4 and 5. Let me also mention that you can exert quite a bit of control over how NT divvies up your computer's resources when you're running more than one program, and Chapter 10 describes how you can do this.

CHAPTER 3

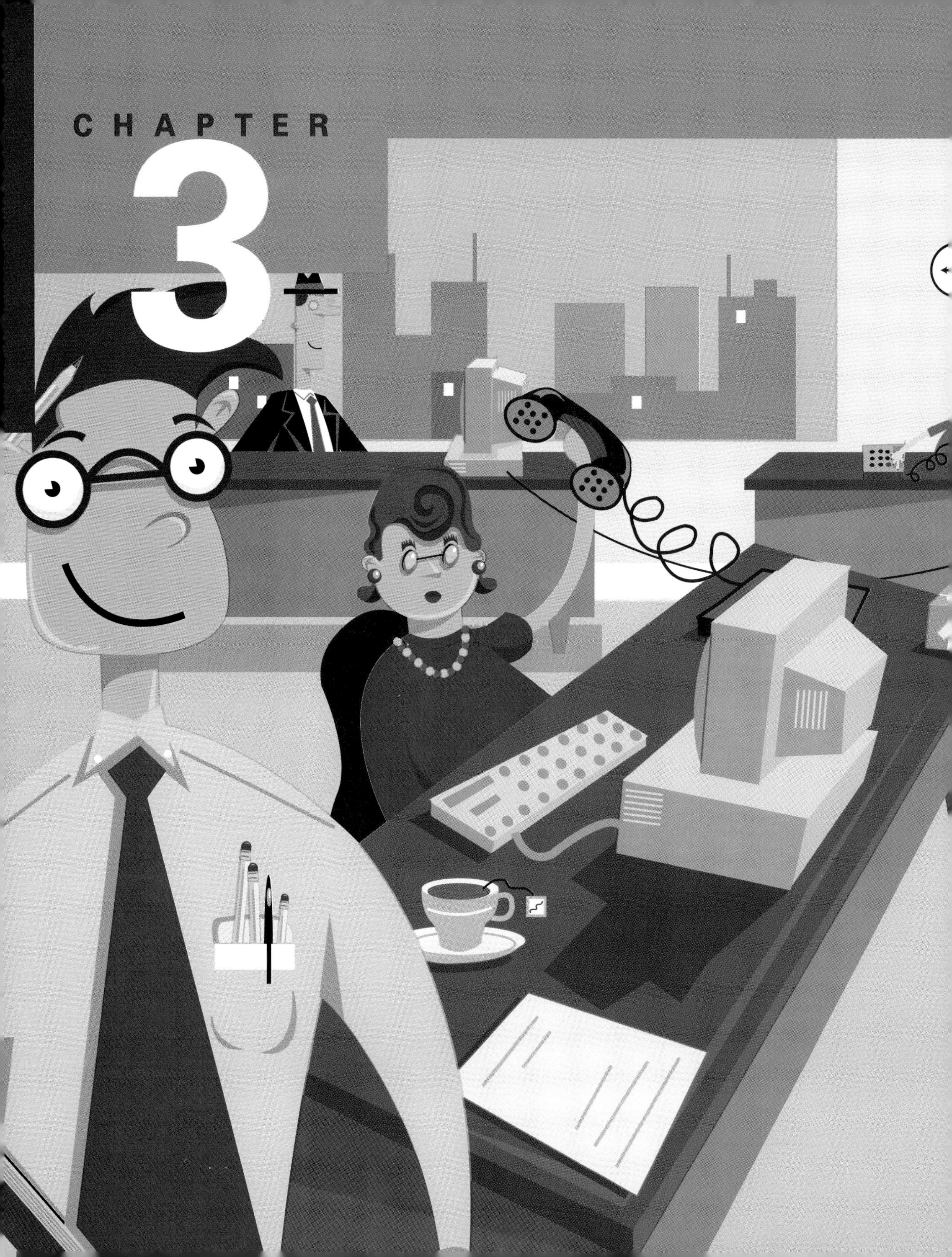

Windows, Commands, and Dialog Boxes

INCLUDES

- Moving windows

- Resizing, hiding, and closing windows

- Choosing menu commands

- Working with dialog boxes

- Using toolbars

- Using shortcut, or context, menus

- Using online help

FAST FORWARD

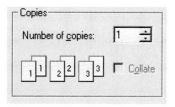

MOVE WINDOWS ➤ *p. 37*

To move a program or document window, drag the window's title bar.

RESIZE, HIDE, AND CLOSE WINDOWS ➤ *pp. 37-38*

Use the Hide button, the Maximize/Restore button, and the Close button to hide, resize, and close program and document windows. You can also drag the window's resize box or the window's border to change its size.

CHOOSE MENU COMMANDS ➤ *pp. 38-39*

To issue a menu command to a program, click the menu so that the program displays the menu and then click the command you want the program to execute.

WORK WITH DIALOG BOXES ➤ *pp. 40-44*

Click check boxes to mark and unmark them. Click an option button or command button to select it. Select a text box and begin typing to enter information into it. To select a list box entry, activate the list box by clicking its arrow and then click the list entry. Drag a slider button to adjust its setting.

USE TOOLBARS ➤ *pp. 45-46*

Click a toolbar's buttons and boxes to use its tools.

USE SHORTCUT, OR CONTEXT, MENUS ➤ *pp. 46-47*

Right-click an object to display a shortcut menu of commands you can use to manipulate the clicked object.

GET HELP ➤ *pp. 47-50*

To tap NT's help feature, click the Start button and choose the Help command. Use the Help program's three tabs—Contents, Index, and Find—to locate the online help information you want.

33

If you've worked with an earlier version of Windows or the Apple Macintosh, you really don't need to read this chapter. Reading it isn't going to hurt, of course. But you already know most of what it covers.

On the other hand, you may be new to computers, or perhaps you've been working with a computer that doesn't use a so-called graphical user interface (with movable windows and clickable boxes and buttons). For example, maybe your only computer experience is with a PC running MS-DOS or with a computer terminal connected to some monstrously large mainframe computer system. If that's the case, then you should read this chapter. By perusing the material here, you'll learn the mechanics of working with Windows NT.

Some people call programs applications *and program windows* application windows.

WINDOWS, WINDOWS EVERYWHERE

Okay, here's the first thing you need to know. NT displays two types of windows: program windows and document windows. *Program windows* appear when you start a program—such as by choosing a program from the Programs menu. Take a look at Figure 3.1. See that rectangular chunk of information that appears in the middle of the screen? That's the Word program window. Notice that NT uses the name of the program (in this case, Microsoft Word) to label the program window. (This label is called the *title bar.*)

Document windows appear inside of program windows. Take another look at Figure 3.1. See that interior window—that rectangle inside the rectangle? That's a document window. NT uses the name of the document file (My first mystery novel.doc) to label the document window. (Again, this label appears on the title bar.)

Sometimes a document window isn't big enough to show the entire document. My novel is currently right around 300 pages, for example, so only the first part of the first page appears in Figure 3.1. For this reason, NT adds a scroll bar (shown in the next illustration) along

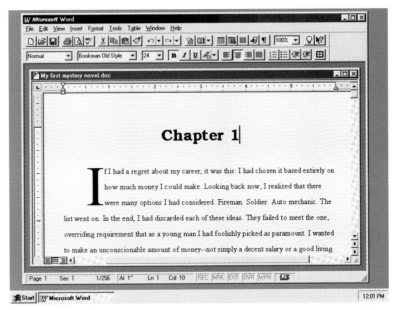

Figure 3.1 The Microsoft Word program window appears in the middle of this screen

the right edge of the document window so I can page through the document.

Drag: *To drag some object, you point to it using the mouse, press and continue holding down the mouse button, and then move the mouse, thereby moving the object. When you finish moving, or dragging, the object, release the mouse button.*

You can use a scroll bar in several ways. You can click the up and down arrows that appear at either end of the scroll bar. You can drag the scroll bar marker up and down (the scroll bar marker is the square that appears on the scroll bar between the arrow buttons). You can also click on the scroll bar itself: click above the scroll bar marker to scroll up, and click below the scroll bar marker to scroll down.

To start Paintbrush, click the Start button. Then choose Programs | Accessories | Paintbrush.

Horizontal scroll bars work like vertical scroll bars, except you move the document left and right instead of up and down. Figure 3.1 shows a horizontal scroll bar, too, because the Word document is wider than the document window.

Moving, Resizing, and Closing Windows

You can do all sorts of fiddling with the windows that NT displays. You can move them, resize them, hide them—the list goes on. Okay, this fiddling may seem like horseplay if you're just starting to use NT. But it's actually pretty handy, because you can arrange program windows on your desktop or document windows inside program windows in any way you want. For example, if your monitor is big enough, you can start two different programs (as described in Chapter 2) and then arrange them so they both show on your screen. As an example, Figure 3.2 shows the Paintbrush program, which comes

SHORTCUT

You can also usually scroll up and sown in a document by pressing the PAGE UP *and* DOWN DN *keys*

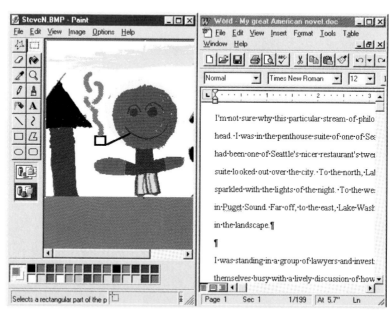

Figure 3.2 You can arrange program windows so that more than one can be viewed at a time

with NT, and a portrait my daughter drew for the dust jacket of my novel (that's why I've got the pipe). The figure also shows the Word program.

Moving Windows

Okay, let's start with window movement first. To move a program or document window, you just drag the window title bar. That's it. Try this if you're not sure about how it works. You should have no trouble.

Resizing, Hiding, and Closing Windows

You can resize windows in one of two ways: by using window buttons or by dragging the mouse. Let's talk window buttons first. In the top right corner of every program window and document window, you'll see three buttons: the Hide button, the Maximize/Restore button, and the Close button. These three buttons let you change the size of the window with a single click. For example, you can click the Hide button to hide a window.

title bar: *The* title bar *appears at the top of a program or document window.*

You can click the Maximize button to increase a program window so it fills the entire screen or a document window so it fills the entire program window.

If you've already maximized a window, Windows NT replaces the Maximize button with the Restore button. You click the Restore button to restore a maximized window to its original size.

In effect, then, Restore unmaximizes a window (I think I'm making up words at this point, but you understand what I mean, right?).

Because we're on the subject of window buttons, I might as well also mention again the Close button even though Chapter 2 describes it too. You can click the Close button to remove a document window from the program window or a program window from the desktop.

If the Close button's operation sounds rather final, it's because it is. When you close a document window, you close the document file shown inside the window. (Typically, the program asks if you want to save any changes you've made to the document.) When you close a program window, you close, or stop, the program.

You can also resize a window by dragging its borders or by dragging the resize box in the lower-right corner of the window. Unfortunately, while the mechanics of resizing are very easy, describing them in a book isn't. So here's what I need you to do. Start a program. It doesn't matter which one. And we'll use that program to illustrate the mechanics.

Ready? Good. Let's try the resize box first. In the lower-right corner of any window that isn't maximized, you'll see the resize box.

If you already maximized the window, click the Restore button to unmaximize it.

Drag the resize box up, down, left, or right. Notice how it changes the window's size by simultaneously changing both the right and bottom borders of the window.

You can also drag a window border to change the window size. To do this, just drag the border. For example, if you want to make the window wider (or more narrow), drag its right border to the right (or to the left). If you want to make the window taller (or shorter), drag its bottom border down (or up).

WORKING WITH MENUS AND COMMANDS

When you want a program to do something, you issue a command. For example, if you want a program to quit, or stop, you issue the Exit command. If you want to print some document, you issue the Print command. You get the idea.

In NT programs, you issue commands in a couple of different ways. One way is to choose a command from a menu, which is simply a list of commands. Another way is to click a toolbar button. If you've never worked with menus and commands before, this can all seem rather perplexing. But you're going to be laughing about how simple this all is in a few minutes, I promise you.

Your First Menu Command

Learning how menu commands work is easy if you follow along at your computer. To do this, click the Start button. Then click the Programs item, click the Accessories item, click the Games item, and finally, click the Solitaire item. When you do this, Windows NT starts the Solitaire program (see Figure 3.3), a highly effective way to waste hours of your time or your employer's time—but also a good way to learn about command mechanics.

If NT's games aren't installed on your computer, you'll need to have them installed by the administrator (which is a very reasonable request, since games are a great way to learn about NT). Or, you'll need to just read this section rather than follow along at your computer.

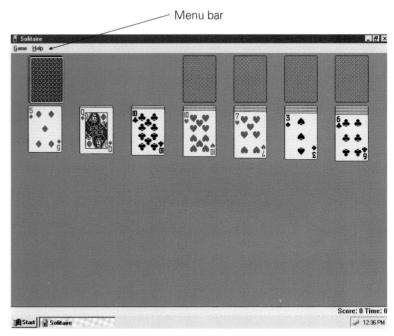

Figure 3.3 Solitaire, like many other programs, lists its menus across the top of the program window, immediately below the program window title bar

39

definition

menu bar: *Most windows programs list their menus across the top of the program window in the* menu bar, *immediately below the program window title bar.*

To issue a menu command to a program, click the menu so that the program displays the menu:

Next, click the command you want the program to execute. For example, to tell Solitaire to redeal the deck, click the Deal command. After you issue the command, Solitaire executes it.

You can also issue commands by using the keyboard, which is usually faster once you know a program well. To use a keyboard, press the ALT key (this activates the menu), press the underlined letter in the menu name (to drop down the menu), and then press the underlined letter in the command name to select the command. To choose the Deal command, for example, press ALT-G-D.

Working with Dialog Boxes

Many times, a program easily carries out the commands you issue. In the case of a command to redeal a deck of playing cards, a program like Solitaire needs no help or additional information from you. But sometimes you must provide additional direction to the program. When this is the case, the program displays a dialog box when you choose the command. You use the dialog box to describe in additional detail how the program should execute the command. Does this make sense? Let me explain.

The Deck command on Solitaire's Game menu tells Solitaire that you want to use a different deck of cards. Solitaire provides several decks of cards, each with a different design on the backs of the cards. So, when you issue the Deck command, Solitaire needs to know which new deck of cards you want. To get this information, it displays the Select Card Back dialog box (see Figure 3.4). To pick the deck you want, click it (this tells Solitaire which deck you want to use).

You can identify which commands display dialog boxes by looking at the menu. Following the command name on the menu, you'll see three periods, or an ellipsis (...).

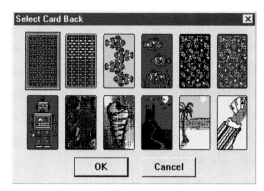

Figure 3.4 The Select Card Back dialog box

When you've provided the extra information that the program needs to complete the command, you click the dialog box's OK command button. This tells Solitaire you've provided the information it needs to carry out the command. Alternatively, you can click the Cancel command button if you want to close the dialog box and cancel the command. By the way, some dialog boxes provide other command buttons. You'll often see a Help command button, for example, which if clicked provides help information. And you'll encounter other command buttons.

Common Dialog Box Elements

Figure 3.4 shows a dialog box that's pretty simple. But sometimes you can't provide the information a program needs simply by clicking a single button (or, in the case of the Select Card Deck dialog box, by clicking an image). So close the Solitaire window—remember, you can do this by clicking its Close button.

Next, let's start the WordPad accessory by clicking the Start button and then choosing Programs | Accessories | WordPad. Once WordPad starts, choose the File | Print command. WordPad displays the Print dialog box shown in Figure 3.5. It shows a check box, option buttons, list box, and text box.

Just below the Properties command button in Figure 3.5, you can see the Print to file check box. *Check boxes* work like on-off switches. When the check box is marked, the "switch" is on. When the check

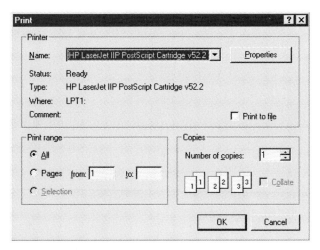

Figure 3.5 The Print dialog box

box is unmarked, the switch is off. To mark and unmark a check box, you click it with your mouse. If your mouse isn't working, you can press the ALT key and the underlined letter in the check box label. (This might be useful information if you're on an airplane 35,000 feet above the Atlantic Ocean and the guy in the next seat isn't keen about you using his meal tray for your mouse.) So, with the dialog box shown in Figure 3.5, you can also press ALT-L to mark and unmark the check box. Go ahead and try this if you're following along at your computer.

Option buttons, another common dialog box element, represent sets of mutually exclusive choices. In Figure 3.5, for example, look at the Print range option buttons—All, Pages, and Selection. You make a choice by marking one of the buttons. When you mark one of the buttons, you also indirectly unmark the previously marked button. To mark a new option, click its button. Or, press the ALT key and the underlined letter in the option button label. For example, to select the All option button in the Print range options, press ALT-A.

A *list box* presents a set of choices. You make your choice, predictably enough, by selecting an item from the list. For example, Figure 3.5 uses the Name list box (in the Printer section) to present a list of printer choices. You can't see the list's entries at first, however, because the list hasn't yet been dropped down. To drop down a list, click the down arrow that appears at the right end of the list box:

When the list appears, select the choice you want. For example, to select the HP LaserJet IIP PostScript Cartridge entry, just click it.

Text boxes are just input blanks that you fill in with a bit of data the program needs. In Figure 3.5, for example, two text boxes—labeled from: and to:—follow the Pages option button. As you can probably guess, you use these text boxes to specify what pages you want to print. To fill a text box, click the box and then type whatever you want entered. Easy, right?

Let me also direct your attention to the Number of copies: text box. If a text box accepts numeric values—as does this text box—the program displaying the dialog box often supplies up and down arrow buttons at the right end of the text box. You can click these arrows to incrementally adjust the text box value. Or, you can type a value.

Sometimes a box works both like a list box and a text box. In other words, you can enter a value directly into the box (so it's part text box). Or you can drop down a list and select a list entry (so it's part list box). These hybrid boxes are called *combo boxes*. You'll see them frequently.

Tabs and Sliders

I should mention a couple of other common dialog box elements, too, before we finish up this discussion: dialog box tabs and slider buttons. The dialog box in Figure 3.5 doesn't show either of these elements, however, so I need you to close the Print dialog box and then the WordPad program window. (Remember, you can easily do this by clicking their Close buttons.)

What I need you to do next is display the Control Panel's Display tool. (I'll talk about the Display tool and the other Control Panel tools in Chapter 7.) To do this, click the Start button. Choose the Settings command from the Start menu. And then choose the Control Panel command from the Settings menu. When Windows NT displays the Control Panel window, double-click the Display tool:

Display

SHORTCUT

You can move from one dialog box element to the next dialog box element by pressing the TAB *key. You can move to the previous dialog box element by pressing* SHIFT-TAB.

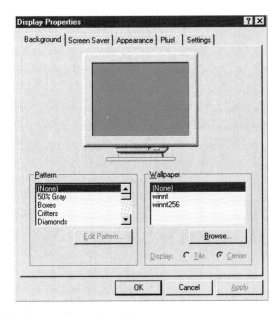

Figure 3.6 The Display Properties dialog box

When you double-click the tool, the Display Properties dialog box appears. Figure 3.6 shows the Display Properties dialog box.

The first thing to notice about the Display Properties dialog box is that it uses tabs. See them? Near the top of the dialog box, you see five tabs labeled Background, Screen Saver, Appearance, Plus!, and Settings. In essence, tabs segregate dialog box options onto different pages when there isn't enough room for them all to appear at the same time. To move to a tab, you just click on it. Try clicking the Settings tab, for example, if you're following along at your computer. Figure 3.7 shows the Settings tab of the Display Properties dialog box.

In the lower-right quarter of the screen, you see a Desktop Area slider button. To use a slider button, you just drag it with the mouse. The Desktop Area slider button, just so you know, lets you adjust the resolution of your monitor. Go ahead and experiment with this. But when you're done, click the Cancel command button to close the Display Properties dialog box without making any changes.

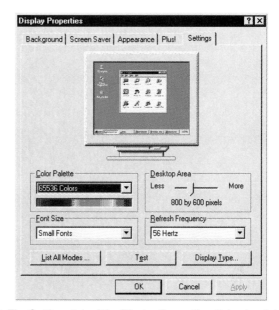

Figure 3.7 The Settings tab of the Display Properties dialog box lets you change the number of colors used for your monitor and its resolution

USING TOOLBARS

Toolbars are those rows of clickable buttons and boxes that appear beneath the menu bar of many programs. Take a look at Figure 3.8. It shows the Microsoft Word for Windows 95 (version 7) program window. You know what the title bar is. You know what the menu bar is. See those two rows of buttons and boxes beneath the menu bar? Those rows are toolbars.

Okay, I know this sounds silly to say, but get into the habit of using toolbars. They almost always save you time. For a single mouse click, for example, you save yourself several mouse clicks or keystrokes. Every toolbar that's worthy of its name, for example, includes a Print button that lets you print a document with a single mouse click. And that's always faster than activating the File menu, choosing the Print command, and then clicking the OK command button.

When you click a toolbar tool, the program typically executes the appropriate command using all of the default dialog box settings. For

Toolbars

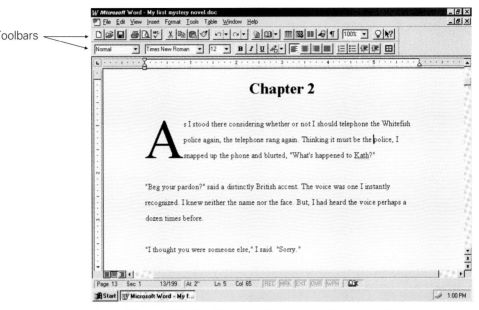

Figure 3.8 The Word for Windows 95 program window provides two toolbars: a standard toolbar and a formatting toolbar

example, if you click the Print tool, the program just prints the document in the usual way: a single copy of the entire document using the default printer.

USING SHORTCUT MENUS

One of the problems with menus is that they list too many commands. If you're working with a popular word processor, for example, it'll probably supply a Format menu with more than a dozen commands. And while that may make the program seem powerful or useful, the jam-packed menu actually reduces your effectiveness. You'll constantly find yourself hunting around for the right command.

Fortunately, some time ago software companies got smart. In effect, they said, "Gee, if some user selects some thingamajig on the screen (say it's a word in a word processor document), we know which commands make sense for the thingamajig...so why don't we create some clever way of displaying only those commands?"

CAUTION

By default, right-clicking an object displays a shortcut menu because left-clicking the mouse is used for other actions such as clicking buttons.

definition

Shortcut Menu: *These list only those commands that are available to act upon the selected object. You simultaneously select the object and display the shortcut menu by right-clicking the object.*

Everybody apparently pondered this idea for a while, agreed it seemed like a good idea, and then started providing shortcut, or context, menus, which appear whenever a user right-clicks some object on the screen. (When you right-click an object, you just use the mouse's right button to click rather than the usual, left button.)

To get an idea of how slick shortcut menus are, reflect on the lengthy set of steps to access the Display Properties dialog box (which we discussed earlier in this chapter): You click the Start button. Then you click the Settings menu item. Then you click the Control Panel menu item. Then you double-click the Display tool. Tedious, right? What you could have done, however—and should do next time, of course—is simply right-click the Windows NT desktop. When you do, Windows NT displays the following shortcut menu:

If you choose the Properties command, Windows NT displays the same Display Properties dialog box that appears in Figures 3.6 and 3.7.

I feel kind of sheepish beating the "shortcut menus are cool" drum. And I'll close the discussion with this paragraph. But I urge you to get into the habit of right-clicking the objects you see on the screen. You'll learn more about the programs you use. And you'll save scads of time. Enough said.

HELP!

NT comes with a rather clever online help feature. If you're sitting in front of your computer and it's on, then with a couple of mouse clicks you can be reading helpful information about all sorts of stuff: Connecting to the Internet. Getting your darn printer working. Finding a missing document.

definition

task bar: *This is the bar along the bottom of the screen that shows the Start button and any task bar buttons for programs you've started.*

To tap NT's help feature, click the Start button and choose the Help command. NT starts the Help program and displays the Help program window (shown in Figure 3.9). The Help program provides three ways to find the information you need: the Contents tab, the Index tab, and the Find tab.

The Contents tab provides a table of contents for all the stuff contained in the help information files. Initially, the Contents tab displays the major categories of help information. To choose one of the categories, click the little book icon to the left of the category. When you click one of these major help categories, you get a list of subcategories. Click a subcategory, and you get a list of topics as shown in Figure 3.10.

By the way, the Help program uses three icons in the Contents tab. The closed book indicates a major help topic category which isn't showing its help topics. The open book indicates a major help topic category that is showing its help topics. The question mark identifies an actual help topic.

If you click an actual topic, the Help program displays either a window of specific help information (in which case, you just read the

Figure 3.9 The Help program window

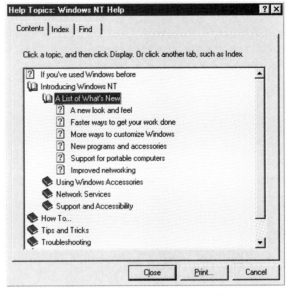

Figure 3.10 The Contents tab after expanding the table of contents

window's text) or a window that provides another list of help topics (in which case, you click the appropriate square button to get the information you need).

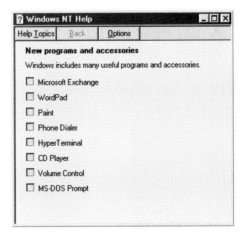

SHORTCUT

To return to the Help program window, click the Help Topics button on the menu bar.

The Index tab provides another way to get to the information you need (see Figure 3.11). The Help index works like the index for this book—almost. You enter the term you want to look up. Help prepares a list of index entries that use the term. You then double-click the index entry to display a program window with help information.

I'm not going to show a picture of the Find tab here, because it works in a manner very similar to that of the Index. You enter a term

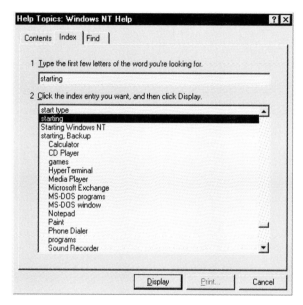

Figure 3.11 The Index tab provides another way to get online help information

you want to learn more about. Help then displays a list of help topics that use the term. You then double-click the help topics you want to read. (If you have the time, do experiment with the Find tab. It's pretty neat.)

ON FROM HERE

You know how to start NT and its programs and how to work with the windows, commands, and dialog boxes you'll encounter. Congratulations. You're ready to begin doing some real work. Chapter 4 describes how you work with documents and disks in NT.

CHAPTER

4

Working with Documents and Disks

INCLUDES

- Viewing a disk's contents

- Opening files

- Deleting and undeleting files

- Renaming files and folders

- Copying and moving files

- Formatting floppy disks

- Monitoring disk space

- Sharing disks

- Exploring a network

- Mapping network drives

FAST FORWARD

VIEW A DISK'S CONTENTS ➤ *pp. 58-60*
Start My Computer by double-clicking its shortcut icon. Then double-click a disk's icon to see the folders, or directories, you've used to organize a disk and the files, or documents, stored in those folders.

OPEN FILES ➤ *pp. 60-61*
If you can display a file in the My Computer or the Network Neighborhood window, you can open the file by double-clicking its icon. If the file is a document, NT starts the appropriate program and then directs it to open the file. If the file is a program, NT starts the program.

DELETE AND UNDELETE FILES ➤ *p. 61*
To delete a file, select it using the My Computer or Network Neighborhood window; then press the DEL key. To undelete a file, display the Recycle Bin by double-clicking its shortcut icon, select the file, and then choose the File menu's Restore command.

RENAME FILES AND FOLDERS ➤ *pp. 61-62*
To rename a file or folder, first display the My Computer or Network Neighborhood window that shows the file or folder. Select the item, then click the file name. When My Computer or Network Neighborhood opens a text box over the file name, type the new name you want to use for the file.

COPY AND MOVE FILES ➤ *pp. 62-63*
To copy and move files, first display a window with the folder holding the file you want to copy or move and a window with the folder to which you want to copy or move the file. To move a file, drag it from the folder it's in to the one you want it to be in. Or, to make a copy of a file, press the CTRL key and then drag it from the folder it's in to the one you want it to be in.

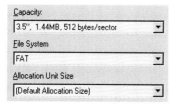

FORMAT FLOPPY DISKS ➤ *pp. 63-64*

Insert the floppy disk you want to format into the floppy disk drive. Next, start the My Computer program. When NT displays the first My Computer window, right-click on the floppy disk icon to display its shortcut menu. Then choose the Format command.

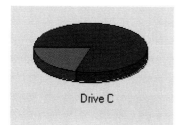

Drive C

MONITOR DISK SPACE ➤ *pp. 64-65*

Start the My Computer program. Right-click the disk you're curious about to display its shortcut menu; then choose its Properties command. When NT displays the disk's Properties dialog box, click its General tab to see a pie chart that shows the amount of disk space you still have free.

SHARE DISKS ➤ *p. 66*

Start the My Computer program. Display the disk or folder you want to share. Right-click the disk or folder to display the shortcut menu and choose the Sharing command. When NT displays the Properties dialog box for the disk or folder, click the Sharing tab. Mark the Shared As option button to indicate this disk or folder should be shared.

Network Neighborhood

EXPLORE A NETWORK ➤ *pp. 67-68*

Use the Network Neighborhood program to view the computers and disks of a network. To start the Network Neighborhood, double-click on the Network Neighborhood shortcut icon.

d$ on 'Gopher' (H:)

MAP NETWORK DRIVES ➤ *pp. 68-70*

Click the Map Network Drive tool, which appears on the Network Neighborhood toolbar and on the My Computer toolbar. When NT displays the Map Network Drive dialog box, use it to specify which disk drive letter NT should use to represent the soon-to-be-mapped network drive and to provide the computer name and the shared drive name.

When all is said and done, it's not the clock speed of your microprocessor that's important. Or which version of some software program you own. It's your data—the documents—that you and the programs you work with store on your hard disk. Business plans. Correspondence with customers or vendors, friends and family. So—and you know this intuitively already—you need to learn how to work with these document files: how to move them around (to more convenient locations, say), how to copy them, give them descriptive names (or new names), and how to delete them when you're done. This chapter describes all this, and more.

NT, like all operating systems, actually stores two types of files on your documents: document files, which I'll refer to here as documents, *and program files, which I'll refer to here as* programs. *I'll use the term* file *to refer to both types of files.*

USING MY COMPUTER

First things first. You have a couple of options as to how you work with your files and disks: the Windows NT Explorer (which I won't talk about here but will briefly describe in Chapter 9) and My Computer (which I will talk about here). My Computer—a funny name, I'll agree— amounts to a "lite" version of the NT Explorer. It does almost everything the regular NT Explorer does, and it's also easy to use, especially for new users.

What is My Computer? Good question. The My Computer program lets you view the devices connected to your computer, the disks and other storage devices you're using, and the stuff you've stored on those disks and storage devices, as shown in Figure 4.1.

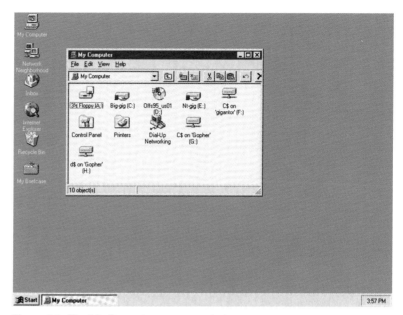

Figure 4.1 The My Computer program window

Starting My Computer

To start My Computer, double-click the My Computer shortcut icon, which appears on the Windows NT Desktop:

After My Computer starts, you see the My Computer program window on your screen (refer to Figure 4.1 again). This window uses icons to represent the different disks connected to your computer (including any network disks). It also shows two folders: the Control

Chapter 7 describes how you use the Control Panel and some of its most useful tools. Chapter 5 describes how you work with the Printers folder.

Panel folder (which provides a bunch of tools you use for tinkering with your computer's operation) and the Printers folder (which describes the printers connected to your computer and any of the documents that those printers are supposed to be printing).

Viewing a Disk's Contents

You can see the folders, or directories, you've used to organize a disk and view the files, or documents, stored in those folders by double-clicking a disk's icon. For example, notice the icon for Big-gig shown in Figure 4.1 (for fun, I named my desktop computer's 1.2 gigabyte disk "Big-gig"). If that icon is clicked, then My Computer displays a new window showing the contents of Big-gig (see Figure 4.2).

Two types of icons fill the window shown in Figure 4.2: folder icons and file icons. The icons that sort of look like manila folders represent each of the folders, or directories, you or some program has created. The other icons represent program and document files.

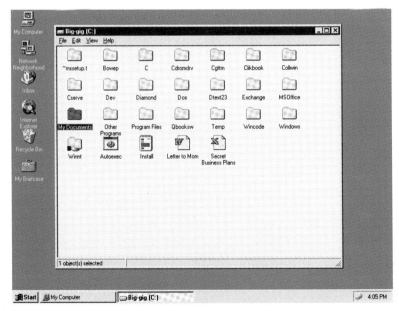

Figure 4.2 This window shows the contents of the 1.2 gigabyte disk on my desktop computer, a disk I fondly call "Big-gig"

58

A folder, or directory, organizes files and other folders. For example, here's the folder named My Documents:

My Documents

If the folder is clicked, another window appears—this one showing the folders (called subfolders) and the files, or documents, within the My Documents folder.

My Computer is pretty smart about the way it displays file icons. If My Computer knows which program was used to create a file, it uses the program's icon as part of the file's icon. This sounds complicated, but take another look at the document icon that follows. See how the icon for the Secret Business Plans file shows a big "X":

Secret
Business Plans

That's the Microsoft Excel icon. By tacking it onto the file icon, My Computer identifies Microsoft Excel as the program I used to create the file and the program that I will need to work with the file.

Notice how the next icon for the Letter to Mom file shows a big "W":

Letter to Mom

That's the Microsoft Word icon. My Computer tacks a "W" onto the file icon to identify Word as the program I used to create the file and the program that I'll use to work with the file.

Let me mention a couple more things. First of all, My Computer doesn't close one window when it opens another one—unless you specifically tell it to by clicking the Close box. Therefore, if you want to view the contents of another disk, you can click the My Computer button on the task bar:

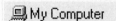

Then, to find the folder or file you want, start the process of searching through a disk's folders all over again.

Here's one other thing you should know. Not all of the icons you'll see in the My Computer window represent folders and files. Windows NT uses icons to represent printers, for example (I'll talk more about printers and printing in Chapter 5).

TI Micro on
GOPHER

And if you keep your eyes open, you'll see a handful of other icons used to represent things like special network connections. This book doesn't talk about esoteric network connections, however.

Doing Stuff with Files

Once you know how to look at the contents of the disks connected to your computer, you're ready to begin working with those files: opening them, deleting them, renaming them, copying them, and so forth.

Opening Files

Let's start with the most useful piece of information first: opening files. If you can display a file in the My Computer window, you can open the file by double-clicking its icon. For example, if you double-click on a word processor document file, NT starts the word processor program you

CAUTION

If you rename or move a program file, you may not be able to use (or at least easily use) the program. And, of course, if you delete a program file, you won't be able to use it at all.

used to create the document and then tells that program to open the file. If you open a program file, NT starts the program.

Deleting and Undeleting Files

If you can find and display a file, or document, in the My Computer window, you can easily delete it. First, right-click it. Then choose the Delete command from the shortcut menu. If it isn't easy to right-click (say, because you're working on a laptop with a pointing device designed by a sadist), you can also just click it and press the DEL key.

You usually can undelete a file—as long as you don't wait too long. Here's how. If you look at the icons displayed on the Windows NT desktop, you'll see one entitled Recycle Bin:

The Recycle Bin amounts to a temporary holding bin for all of the files you've deleted. There isn't unlimited room in the Recycle Bin. You can't store all your deleted files there for all time. But all of your most recently deleted files appear there.

To undelete a previously deleted file, you first display the contents of the Recycle Bin. To do this, double-click the Recycle Bin shortcut icon. When My Computer displays a window showing the Recycle Bin's contents, find the file you want to undelete, right-click it, and choose the Restore command from the shortcut menu. My Computer (with the help of NT) undoes your deletion, placing the file back into its original folder.

Renaming Files and Folders

You easily can rename a file or folder. First display the My Computer window that shows the file or folder. Select the item and then click the file name. My Computer opens a text box over the file name:

habits & strategies

If you want to free up additional disk space and you know you'll never want to undelete the files stored in the Recycle Bin, display the Recycle Bin window and then choose its File | Empty Recycle Bin command.

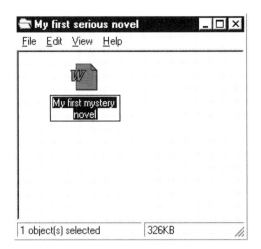

You then type the name you want to use for the file. You can use letters, numbers, spaces, and most special characters in your name. There are a handful of characters you can't use, but I'm not going to list them here. There's no reason to. You might not remember what I tell you. And if you do try to use an illegal character (such as a slash or a colon), My Computer will just tell you that what you've done isn't kosher anyway.

By the way, you can rename folders in the same way that you rename files. You display the folder's icon in the My Computer window. Select the folder and click the folder name. When My Computer opens a text box over the folder name, you type the new name you want to use.

Copying and Moving Files

Copying and moving files are easy once you know how to use My Computer to display the contents of folders. Here's what you do: First, display a window with the folder holding the file you want to copy or move. Next, display a second window with the folder to which you want to copy or move the file. Figure 4.3 shows two windows arranged just this way.

To move a file, drag it from the folder where it is located to the one you want it to be in. Or, to make a copy of a file, press the CTRL key and then drag the file from the folder it's in to the one where you want

If you drag a file to a floppy disk's folder (without holding down the CTRL *key), My Computer doesn't move the file. It copies the file.*

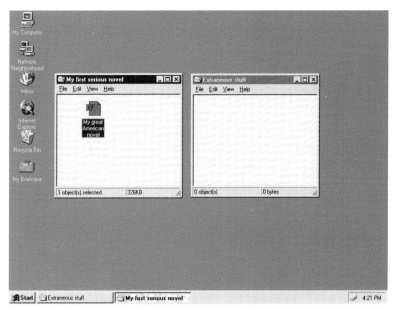

Figure 4.3 If you display windows for both the source and destination folders, it's easy to copy and move files between folders

it located. (You may want to rename the copy after you do this—just so you don't get the two files confused.)

MANAGING YOUR DISKS

As you work with NT, you'll need to know how to perform three disk management tasks: how to format floppy disks (yes, you'll still use these), how to monitor the free space on your hard disk (and any other disks), and how to share a disk so other network users can get to it—and use its information.

Formatting Floppy Disks

Even when you're on a network, you'll still use floppy disks to move files from one computer to another. For example, you might want to bring a file home with you to work on over the weekend. Or you might want to send a document—by mail, say—to others so they can work on it. For these reasons, you'll still find yourself formatting floppy disks.

SHORTCUT

To quickly reformat a floppy disk, mark the Quick Format check box. Don't worry, however, about the other options and buttons in the Format Disk dialog box. These don't matter when you're formatting floppy disks.

Fortunately, formatting a floppy disk with NT is easy. Insert the floppy disk you want to format into the floppy disk drive. Next, start the My Computer program. When NT displays the first My Computer window (see Figure 4.1), right-click on the floppy disk icon to display its shortcut menu. Then choose the Format command. NT displays the Format Disk dialog box, shown in Figure 4.4.

Use the Capacity drop-down list box to specify the floppy disk type and density: 5.25 inch 360K, 5.25 inch 1.2MB, 3.5 inch 720MB, 3.5 inch 1.44MB, and so on. If you're unsure how you're supposed to know this, just refer to the box that the floppy disks came in. Or, in a pinch, measure the disk with a ruler to determine its size and then experiment with the two density options for your size floppy disk. NT can't format a disk using the wrong capacity specification, so you can experiment with different settings until you get one that works.

To begin the formatting, click Start. NT formats the disk. When it finishes, it displays a message box telling you it's done. Click OK to close this message box, and then click the Close button in the Format Disk dialog box to remove the dialog box from the screen.

Monitoring Disk Space

Unless you've got a lot bigger hard disk than you need, you'll want to regularly monitor the available disk space on your computer. You

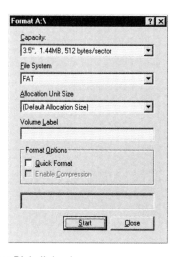

Figure 4.4 The Format Disk dialog box

don't want to find yourself coming up short at some critical juncture—like right before you're supposed to assemble some huge document that uses a bunch of space-hungry graphic images. What's more, NT likes to use a certain amount of disk space as fake, or virtual, memory.

Monitoring disk space isn't a problem, however. Start the My Computer program. Right-click the disk you're curious about (so NT displays the shortcut menu). And then choose the Properties command. NT displays the disk's Properties dialog box (see Figure 4.5). It uses a pie chart to show you the amount of disk space you've used and the amount of disk space you still have free.

Unfortunately, I don't have some magic bullet for you if you find your disk is almost full. You've really only got three options:

- You can move files to another disk (described earlier in the chapter).
- You can delete files you don't need (also described earlier).
- Or you can have someone add a hard disk to your computer for probably $300 to $400. I find myself adding hard disks to computers all the time, because the operating systems and programs are getting bigger and the amount of information that I've got stored on my computer grows over time.

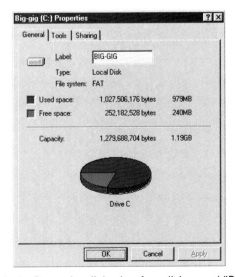

Figure 4.5 This is the Properties dialog box for a disk named "Big-gig"

administrator: *A user who can*

make changes to the security

settings of the network,

including changing passwords,

sharing disks, and a bunch of

other esoteric stuff.

Sharing Disks

Let me tell you about one other disk management task—although I should say up front that it's one you may not be able to do yourself. You may need the network administrator's help. But let me explain. In order for a disk to be available to the other people using a network, someone with administrator or Power User privileges needs to authorize this sharing.

If you have administrator privileges, you share a disk or folder in the following way. Start My Computer. Display the disk or folder you want to share. Right-click the disk or folder to display the shortcut menu and choose the Sharing command. NT displays the Sharing tab of the Properties dialog box (see Figure 4.6).

Mark the Shared As option button to indicate this disk or folder should be shared. And then accept the suggested share name, which will be the drive letter or folder name. Then click OK.

After you've shared a disk or folder, other network users will be able to map to the disk or folder and then use it. I describe what mapping is and how you do it in the next section of this chapter.

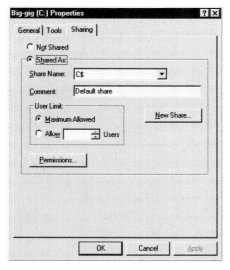

Figure 4.6 The Sharing tab of the disk or folder Properties dialog box

If you don't see the Sharing

command on your shortcut

menu or the Sharing tab on your

Properties dialog box, then

either you don't have adminis-

trator or power user privileges,

or networking is not installed

and you won't be able to share

the disk or folder.

EXPLORING YOUR NETWORK

So far in this chapter, I've talked about the fact that NT is a network operating system. And I've even explained that in order for other network users to get stuff off of your hard disk, your disk must be shared. What I haven't explained thus far, however, is how you grab stuff from other people's computers. So that's what this final section of the chapter does. It explains how you use another program that NT supplies, called Network Neighborhood, to make your life and work easier. If you're not working with Windows NT on a network, go ahead and jump to the "On from Here" section at the end of the chapter.

An Overview of Network Neighborhood

In a nutshell, the Network Neighborhood identifies the pieces and parts of a network: its domains and its computers. *Domains* represent groups of computers that get administered together (typically because they have similar security problems to solve or security issues to deal with). To start the Network Neighborhood, you click on the Network Neighborhood shortcut icon:

After you do this, Windows NT opens the Network Neighborhood window (see Figure 4.7).

The Network Neighborhood will, at the very least, show an icon for the Entire Network. If you've already connected your computer to other computers in a network, it may also show icons for other computers. Figure 4.7, for example, shows an Entire Network icon and a bunch of other icons for desktop computers with names like Gopher, Enola, Gigantor, Nevada, and so forth.

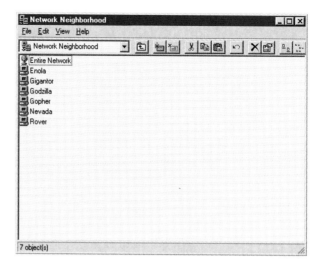

Figure 4.7 The Network Neighborhood window

To display a computer's shared disks (disks that the network administrator has made available to other network users) double-click the computer. Figure 4.8 shows the result of double-clicking the Gigantor icon—you can see the shared disks and folders connected to Gigantor.

Mapping Network Drives

Okay, there is one little twist—one minor complication—in this matter. If you don't see a disk or folder that you know is there and that you know is shared, it's because you need to map the network drive. In other words, you need to tell NT that you want to view a specific disk on a specific computer. The trick here is that you need to first know the computer's name and the shared name of the disk or folder before you can do this. (You'll probably need to get this information from the administrator, since he or she is the one who names computers and disks.) But once you do have this information, you click the Map Network Drive tool, which appears on the Network Neighborhood toolbar:

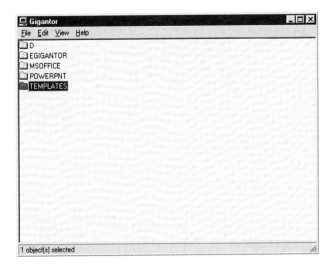

Figure 4.8 The Network Neighborhood window showing the shared disks and folders of the computer named Gigantor

When NT displays the Map Network Drive dialog box, shown in Figure 4.9, you can use it to specify the disk drive letter (which NT will use to represent the soon-to-be-mapped network drive), the computer name, and the shared drive name.

Typically, you will accept the drive letter that NT suggests and shows in the Drive drop-down list box. NT just assigns the next available drive letter to the mapped network drive, and this is probably what you want. For example, in Figure 4.9, NT suggests the letter J be used to represent the next network drive, because I've already used the letters A and B for floppy drives, the letters C, D, and E for hard and CD-ROM drives, and the letters F, G, H, and I for previously mapped network drives.

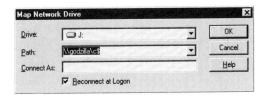

Figure 4.9 The Map Network Drive dialog box

The only tricky part is the information in the Path box. Here you need to enter the computer name and the shared disk name (which is technically called a folder name), using the following form:

\\computername\foldername

For example, if you want to map to the disk named c$ on the computer named rover, you enter **\\rover\c$** in the path box.

The Map Network Drive dialog box also provides two other options: the Connect As box and the Reconnect at Logon check box. You typically shouldn't have to worry about the Connect As box. It lets you connect to a shared disk or folder as some other user. If you want, you can mark the Reconnect at Logon check box. This tells NT to reconnect to the network drive whenever you log on. (This will mean your logon takes slightly longer, but if you're going to be grabbing stuff from a bunch of different network drives, you might as well reconnect to them all at once when you log on and get this work out of the way.)

After you finish specifying how NT should map to the network drive, click OK. NT attempts to find the network drive. If it does, it opens a new window showing the drive's or folder's contents. If it can't find the network drive, it displays an error message. If you get an error message and you're sure that the computer and disk exist, that the disk is shared, and that the network connections are working, then your problem is that you've entered either the computer name or the disk name incorrectly or that you don't have rights to access it.

Working with Network Drives and Folders

Once you display a Network Neighborhood window that shows a shared, mapped disk, you can often work with the disk's files and folders just as if the disk is connected to your computer. (In fact, the disk is connected to your computer by the network.) You can open files, copy and move them, and even delete and undelete them. I described how you do all these tasks earlier in the chapter, so I won't repeat myself here. The key thing to remember is that you can use the Network Neighborhood to view the contents of other computer's disks—just as you use My Computer to view the contents of your computer's disks.

CAUTION

To work with another computer's disks, you need to have the right permissions (something I talk about more in Chapter 6).

ON FROM HERE

Once you know how to effortlessly move around a network, viewing disks and working with files, there actually isn't all that much else you need to learn. Oh sure. You'll benefit by learning how printing works with NT; we'll do that in Chapter 5. And you'll find it helpful to learn a bit more about how NT's security features work, so we'll do this in Chapter 6. But all in all, you now know more than enough to be productive in your work with NT.

CHAPTER

5

CAFE

Printing

INCLUDES

- Understanding how NT prints

- Installing local and network printers

- Printing a document

- Working with a printer and its documents

FAST FORWARD

HP LaserJet
IIP PostScri...

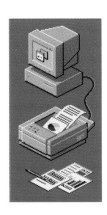

TI Micro on
GOPHER

ADD A LOCAL PRINTER ➤ *p. 77*

To add, or install, a local printer, first display the Printers folder by clicking Start and then choosing the Settings | Printers command. When NT displays the Printers window, double-click the Add Printer Wizard shortcut icon. Then use the dialog boxes that NT displays to describe the printer.

ADD A NETWORK PRINTER ➤ *p. 81*

To add, or install, a network printer, first display the Printers folder by clicking Start and then choosing the Settings | Printers command. When NT displays the Printers window, double-click the Add Printer Wizard shortcut icon. Then use the dialog boxes that NT displays to identify the network printer server and the printer.

PRINT A DOCUMENT ➤ *p. 82*

You can usually print a document by clicking a program's Print tool, which appears on the program's toolbar. When you use the Print tool, NT prints the document with all the default print settings. If you want to exert more control over your printing, choose the program's Print command (usually File | Print) and then use the Print dialog box to describe how NT should print the document.

Document Name
D:\STEFSTUF\Exchange\ExCh B...
Microsoft Exchange: printing
Microsoft Word - NTCHAP05.doc
D:\STEFSTUF\Exchange\ExCh B...

VIEW A PRINTER'S SPOOL FILES ➤ *p. 84*

To work with a printer or view its printer jobs (spool files), you first need to display its window. To do this, click Start. Choose the Settings | Printers command. When NT displays the Printers window, double-click on the printer's icon.

Properties

USE THE DOCUMENT COMMANDS ➤ *pp. 84-85*

Once you're in the printer window, use commands on the Document menu to pause, resume, restart, cancel, and change the printing order of a spool file.

- Choose Pause to temporarily stop a document from printing; later choose Resume to undo the effect of your earlier pause command.
- Choose Restart to tell NT it should start printing a document all over again.
- Choose Cancel to remove a spool file from the print queue.
- Choose Properties to change the print order of the spool file or to schedule when it should print.

You probably will never find it difficult to print a document using NT. In fact, from within most programs, all you've got to do is click a Print toolbar button. Nevertheless, you'll still benefit from understanding a bit more about how printing under NT works and how to work with printers from within NT. With this information, you'll be able to save printing time, and you'll be able to troubleshoot some of the printing problems you encounter.

UNDERSTANDING HOW NT PRINTS

If you've issued several print commands from a program or several programs, NT may be holding several documents in the queue.

Let's start off with a quick discussion of what happens when you tell a program—say it's your word processor—to print. When you issue the print command, roughly four things happen. First, the word processor program hands a copy of the document to NT along with instructions to use a particular printer. Next, NT creates something called a *spool file* (which is basically a printable copy of the document) specifically for the selected printer. When NT finishes creating the printable copy of the document, it places the spool file in a queue to wait its turn to be printed. Finally, when the spool file reaches the front of the line, NT patiently hands off pages to your printer.

This simple description may not seem to contain any earth-shaking information, but take note of a couple of items. First, it's not your application program—the word processor in our little example—that does the printing; it's NT. This means that your programs (like your word processor) don't typically need to know anything about your printer. Only NT needs to know. We'll talk more about this later in the "Working with a Printer" section.

Another item useful to know is that while it's usually your computer that does the work of creating the spool file, you can actually use another computer to create the pages of the spool file and to hand off the pages of the spool file to the printer (such as a really fast network printer just down the hall).

Finally, remember that there is a line, or print queue, of spool files waiting to be printed. Depending on the size and complexity of these spool files, what you think is a printing problem ("Hey, my two-page report won't print!") may really be an etiquette problem ("Hey, Nelson is printing that 800-page report again...that turkey!").

INSTALLING LOCAL AND NETWORK PRINTERS

In order to print a document, NT needs to know which printer you want to use. It also needs information about the printer's technical specifications: what size paper it uses, which printer language it uses (PostScript, PCL, and so on), which fonts it supports, how much memory it has, and a bunch of other stuff as well. Fortunately, you don't need to know any of this. All you need to know is your printer's precise name. Once you know this information, you install the printer by "adding" it to NT's list of printers.

I need to mention one weird aspect of this printer installation business, however. You need to add every printer you want to use—even one that's not connected to your computer. This means that if you want to use a network printer (a printer that's connected to a server or to another user's computer), you need to add the printer to the list on your machine. It doesn't matter if the printer has already been added to the computer that it's physically connected to. For this reason, I'm going to describe how you add both a local printer (one that's connected to your computer) and a network printer (one that's connected to some other computer on the network).

Adding a Local Printer

To add, or install, a local printer, first display the Printers folder. You do this by clicking Start, and then choosing the Settings | Printers command. NT then displays the Printers window:

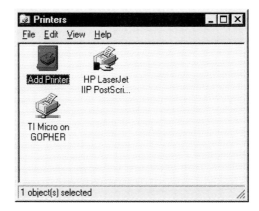

I'm not going to show all of the Add Printer Wizard's dialog boxes here. In many cases, it'll be easier for you to just have me describe them in the text.

This window shows icons for any local or network printers you've already added and a shortcut icon entitled Add Printer Wizard, which runs the printer installation program.

To start the Add Printer Wizard, you double-click its shortcut icon. The printer installation program starts and displays a dialog box that asks its first question: whether the printer connects to your computer or to some other computer (a network printer server). For a local printer, select My Computer and then click Next to move to the next Add Printer Wizard dialog box.

The Add Printer Wizard next displays a dialog box that asks which printer port NT should use for printing to this printer (see Figure 5.1). You won't know this, of course. Who would? But it usually isn't too difficult to find out or guess correctly. You may be able to follow the cable that connects your printer to the back of your computer and read a label next to the port (or socket). In other words, the port may be labeled LPT1 or COM2. If this isn't possible, go ahead and experiment, starting with the first parallel port, LPT1. Or ask for help from the person who installed NT in the first place.

After you specify the printer port, click Next. NT displays the third Add Printer Wizard dialog box (see Figure 5.2). Basically, this one asks you to specifically identify the printer you're installing. To make this identification, use the Manufacturers list box to select the printer maker. Then use the Printers list box to select the printer model.

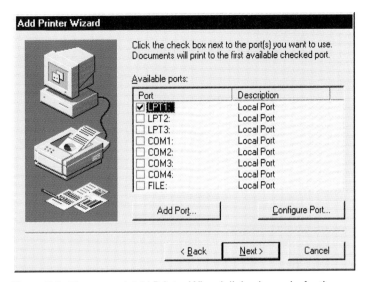

Figure 5.1 The second Add Printer Wizard dialog box asks for the printer port

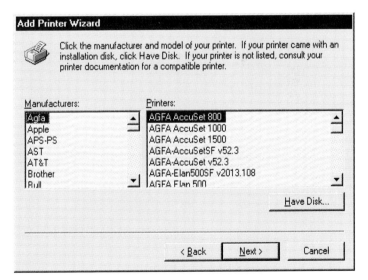

Figure 5.2 The third Add Printer Wizard dialog box asks you to identify your printer

**habits &
strategies**

NT works on more than one type

of computer and so provides

different flavors of its operating

system: x86 for Intel 386

processors (which include

80386, 80486, Pentium, and

Pentium Pro processors),

Alpha for Digital Equipment

Corporation's Alpha chip

processors, and so on.

If you can't find the manufacturer (unlikely) or the model (quite possible, if your printer is brand new), you've got two options. If your printer emulates, or pretends to be, some other printer, you can just tell NT that your printer is this other printer—it won't know the difference. Or, you can get the printer description information that NT needs from a disk provided by the printer manufacturer. In this case, find the disk that came with the printer labeled "Windows NT drivers" (or something like that). Then, click the Have Disk command button and follow the instructions that NT provides in the dialog box that appears.

After you identify the printer manufacturer and printer model, click the Next button to move to the fourth Add Printer Wizard dialog box. This dialog box asks you to name the printer. You use whatever name you want: Joe-Bob, Carol, Knave, or whatever. But it's usually easier (in the long run) to keep track of your printers if you use a name that identifies the printer more precisely. You also use this fourth dialog box to indicate whether you want all of your Windows-based programs to use this printer as the default, or suggested, printer.

After you name the Printer, click the Next button to move to the fifth Add Printer Wizard dialog box (see Figure 5.3). This dialog box asks

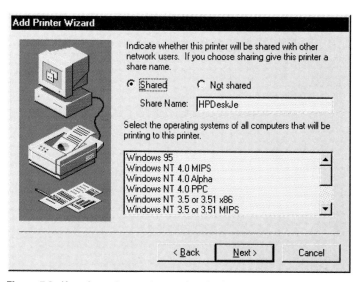

Figure 5.3 If you're going to share a local printer, you need to name the shared printer and identify which operating systems will use the printer

you whether you want to share the printer. If you indicate that you want to share the printer (by clicking the Shared option button), you'll also need to give the shared printer a name (using the Share Name text box) and identify which operating systems and which flavors of NT will use the printer (using the list box provided). Get the administrator's help if you're not sure about the operating systems and flavors of NT in use.

After you indicate whether or not you'll share the printer, click Next. The Add Printer Wizard displays its final dialog box. It simply asks if you want to print a test page. You do, so mark the Yes option button and click Finish. NT prints the test page. After NT prints the test page, it displays another message box asking whether the page printed okay. If you click No, NT's help feature displays a bunch of help information to help you get your printer installed correctly.

And you can get on with the rest of your life.

Adding a Network Printer

Adding a network printer works slightly differently than adding a local printer. You start the Add Printer Wizard program (click Start, choose Settings | Printers, and then double-click the Add Printer Wizard shortcut icon). You indicate that you want to add a printer connected to a network printer server by clicking the appropriate option button on the first Add Printer Wizard dialog box.

In the second Add Printer Wizard dialog box which is actually called the Connect to Printer dialog box (see Figure 5.4), NT asks you to identify the network printer server and the printer. Double-click the network printer server—the computer to which the printer connects, click the printer, and then click OK to move to the next Add Printer Wizard dialog box.

After you successfully identify the printer and click OK, NT displays the third Add Printer Wizard dialog box. It simply asks whether or not you want the network printer you're installing to be the default printer for your Windows-based program. Click either the Yes or No option button to answer this burning question. Then click Next. NT displays a fourth and final Add Printer Wizard dialog box telling you the network printer has been successfully installed. Click Finish, and you're done.

habits & strategies

After you identify the printer, the Add Printer Wizard may prompt you for the NT installation CD or one of the NT installation floppy disks. It does this when it needs to retrieve information about the printer and can't get that information from the network printer server.

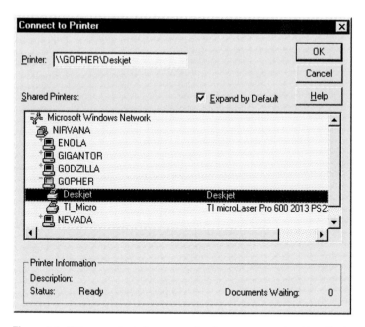

Figure 5.4 When you install a network printer, you need to identify the printer server and the printer

PRINTING A DOCUMENT

Once you've got your printer or printers installed, printing documents is really easy. In many programs, all you have to do is click the Print tool, which appears on the toolbar. Typically, when you print a document using the Print tool, the program tells NT to print the document with all the default print settings: the usual printer, a single copy, and so forth. I think all the major programs have toolbars with Print tools, but I confess that I haven't painstakingly reviewed all 87 programs.

If you want to exert more control over your printing, you'll want to print using a command. Typically, you do this using the File | Print command. Figure 5.5 shows the Print dialog box that Word displays when you choose the File | Print command; it's representative of a typical Print dialog box, so let's take a couple of minutes and talk about it.

On most Print dialog boxes, you'll see a group of settings related to the printer. Initially, these settings will show whatever printer you've selected as your default printer. But you can usually select another installed printer. In the Print dialog box shown in Figure 5.5, for example,

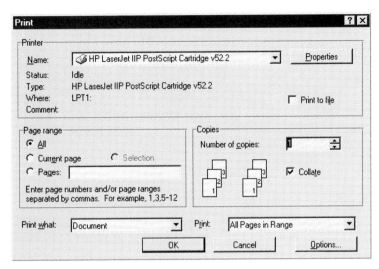

Figure 5.5 Microsoft Word's Print dialog box looks and works very much like the Print dialog boxes in other programs

habits & strategies

If you have questions about a button or box on your Print dialog box, click the question mark button and then click the button or box you have a question about. NT starts its Help program and displays information about whatever you clicked.

you can activate the Name drop-down list box and select any installed local or network printer. You'll also typically see a Properties command button, which lets you change specific properties of the selected printer: page orientation (portrait vs. landscape), paper size, and so on.

Depending on the program you're printing from, you'll often see a bunch of other print settings as well. Word processors, for example, always let you select a range of pages in a document. And you can usually specify that a certain number of copies be printed.

WORKING WITH A PRINTER

Early in this chapter, I mentioned that it's not really your program that prints. It's NT. That bit of information may have seemed irrelevant (and maybe it still is). But because NT prints your documents and is rather formal and ordered about the way it does this, you can exercise quite a bit of control over the way NT prints, such as: when it prints documents, the order in which it prints documents, and *if* it even prints documents.

To work with a printer, you first need to display its window. To do this, click Start. Choose the Settings | Printers command. When NT displays the Printers window, double-click on the printer's icon to tell

NT to open the printer's window. In this example, the following printer icon is double-clicked:

TI Micro on
GOPHER

This is one of our network printers, a Texas Instruments Microlaser Pro 600. Figure 5.6 shows the printer window for it.

The information shown in the printer window may seem like gobbledygook. But it's not. It's really quite useful. For example, just by looking at the printer window in Figure 5.6—specifically the print queue—I know that I can't expect to print anything on that printer soon. There's a 10 megabyte spool file that's currently printing. And right behind that there's another, almost 20 megabyte spool file waiting to print. (These files are Adobe PageMaker desktop publishing files, which is why they're so big.) The itty-bitty spool file listed third – the one identified as the Administrator's—is mine.

Using the Document Commands

Document Name	Status	Owner	Pages	Size	Submitted	Port
D:\STEFSTUF\Exchange\ExCh B...	Printing	STEFANK		7.89MB/10.0MB	5:13:37 AM 5/31/97	LPT2:
Microsoft Exchange: printing		STEFANK		18.9KB	5:30:00 AM 5/31/97	
Microsoft Word - NTCHAP05.doc		Administr...	7	39.8KB	5:34:45 AM 5/31/97	
D:\STEFSTUF\Exchange\ExCh B...		STEFANK		7.24MB	5:40:15 AM 5/31/97	

TI Micro on GOPHER
Printer Document View Help

Figure 5.6 The printer window lists the spool files in a printer's queue

You can do more than look at a printer window, however. If you select a document, you can use the commands on the Document menu: Pause, Resume, Restart, Cancel, and Properties. Choose the Pause command to temporarily stop a document from printing; later choose

CAUTION

NT displays spool files in the order in which they were created, which isn't necessarily the same order in which they'll print. This can be particularly confusing if you start adjusting the print priorities of various jobs.

Resume to undo the effect of your earlier pause command. Choose the Restart command to tell NT it should start printing a document all over again. Choose Cancel to remove a spool file from the print queue.

If you have full access over the printer—a high level of authority—you can also change the order of spool files in the queue. To do this, select the document you want to move and then choose the Document | Properties command. When NT displays the document properties dialog box (Collage Complete Properties, in this case—see Figure 5.7), use the Priority slider button to increase the print priority of the spool file. By default, a spool file's print priority equals 1, so any value higher than 1 moves the selected spool file to the front of the line.

You can also use the document properties dialog box to schedule when a particular spool file should print. This can be really handy. If you've got some lengthy report to print, you can tell NT to print the spool file after the workday ends.

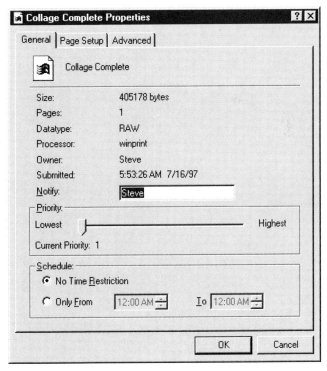

Figure 5.7 The document properties dialog box lets you move a document up or down the print queue

Using the Printer Commands

Unless you're the administrator, you won't have much occasion to work with the printer window's Printer menu commands. Sure, the Pause Printing command stops the printer. And the Purge Print Document command just removes all of the spool files from the print queue. But the rest of the commands are so esoteric that you'll probably never have occasion to fiddle with them. (Because no one else will volunteer, for example, I'm the administrator for our little NT network. And I never mess around with this stuff.)

ON FROM HERE

I don't know if you've sensed it or not, but a recurring topic keeps popping up here and there throughout the early chapters of this book. Every time we (you and I) stumble onto the topic, though, I start dancing around and get vague. But it's time for me to stop fooling around. You need to learn about this topic—how NT's security works—in reasonable detail. So that's what Chapter 6 docs.

CHAPTER

6

Using NT's Security

INCLUDES

- Understanding NT's security tools

- Working with accounts and groups

- Working with rights

- Working with permissions

- Working with audit logs

FAST FORWARD

USE NT'S SECURITY ➤ pp. 93-95

NT provides five security tools: accounts, rights, permissions, groups, and audit logs.

- *Accounts* work like country club memberships.
- *Rights* amount to special privileges.
- *Permissions* control access to specific resources.
- *Groups* simplify the administrator workload.
- *Audit logs* monitor specified activities and events.

CREATE A NEW ACCOUNT ➤ p. 97

To create a new user account, start the User Manager program. Choose the User | New User command. When NT displays the New User dialog box, provide the user name and a password.

EDIT AN EXISTING ACCOUNT ➤ p. 98

To edit some element of an existing account, start the User Manager program. Double-click the user's account. When NT displays the User Properties dialog box, use it to make your changes.

CREATE A GROUP ➤ pp. 98-99

To create a new group, start the User Manager. Select the users you want to add to the new group. Then choose the User | New Local Group command. When NT displays the New Local Group dialog box, name and describe the group.

EDIT AN EXISTING GROUP ➤ pp. 99-100

To edit an existing group's name or description, start the User Manager program. Double-click the group. When NT displays the Local Group Properties dialog box, make your changes and click OK.

SPECIFY ACCOUNT POLICIES ➤ *pp. 100-101*

To set overall account policy for all of the accounts on a computer or network, start the User Manager program. Then choose the Policies | Account command. When NT displays the Account Policy dialog box, use it to describe how passwords should be created and updated and how the logon process should work.

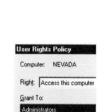

ASSIGN RIGHTS ➤ *pp. 101-102*

To assign rights to groups and user accounts, start the User Manager and choose the Policies | User Rights command. When NT displays the User Rights Policy dialog box, activate the Right drop-down list box and select the right you want to assign to some group. Click the Add button so that NT displays a list of groups and users. Then add users and groups to the list of users and groups that have the right by double-clicking.

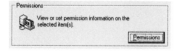

SET SHARE PERMISSIONS
ON A FAT DISK ➤ *pp. 103-106*

To set the share permissions on a FAT disk drive, start My Computer and right-click the disk you want to set share permissions for. In the shortcut menu, choose the Sharing command so that NT displays the Sharing tab of the Properties dialog box. Use it to specify what share permissions you want to give.

SET PERMISSIONS ON
AN NTFS DISK ➤ *pp. 106-108*

To set the permissions on an NTFS disk drive, start My Computer and then display the disk, folder, or file you want to set permissions for. Right-click the item so that NT displays the shortcut menu. Select Properties. When NT displays the Normal Properties dialog box, click the Security tab. Click the Permissions command button so that NT displays the Permissions dialog box. Use it to specify what permissions you want to give.

TI Micro

SET PERMISSIONS ON A PRINTER ➤ pp. 108-110

To set permissions on a local printer, start My Computer and open the Printers folder so that the printer's shortcut icon shows. Right-click the printer so its shortcut menu shows, and then select the Sharing command. When NT displays the printer's Properties dialog box, use it to specify what permissions you want to give.

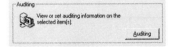

CREATE AUDIT LOGS ➤ pp. 110-111

To create an audit log, start My Computer and then display the resource you want to audit. Right-click the item so that NT displays the shortcut menu. Select Properties. When NT displays the Properties dialog box, click the Security tab. Next, click the Auditing command button so that NT displays the File Auditing dialog box. Use it to specify the printer permissions you want to give.

This chapter discusses the security issues relevant to stand-alone computers and single-domain networks. It doesn't describe the special security issues relevant to multiple-domain networks.

While NT's security features aren't that difficult to understand—or to use—they are its most poorly documented feature. Read what the user documentation has to say about user rights, permissions, and audit logs, and you may find your eyes glazing over and your mind clouding with confusion. This chapter explains in plain English how all this stuff works.

UNDERSTANDING NT'S SECURITY

When you boil everything down to its essence, NT provides five security tools: accounts, rights, permissions, groups, and audit logs. If you understand what these tools are and how they work, everything else falls into place. So I want to start this chapter with a quick explanation of these five tools. No, I'm not going to try turning you into a network administrator. But you do need to understand the conceptual framework of NT's security system.

Accounts Work Like Country Club Memberships

Accounts represent the first security tool—and probably the most important. NT requires that every computer connecting to your network has an account. NT also requires that every person logging in to a computer on the network has an account. You can think about accounts like country club memberships. With a country club membership, you get into the club for golf, tennis, or uninspired dining. With an account, a computer or user gets into the network.

Typically, you never have to worry about computer accounts. If you're connected to a network, the NT installation program creates a computer account when you install NT. (The network administrator can also create a computer account if need be.) What's more, when NT starts, the computer account checking—the so-called "authentication"—that goes on between your computer and the network's computers happens behind the scenes.

User accounts are another matter, however. If you're running NT on a network, the network administrator needs to use a special program, the User Manager, to create your user accounts. When the network administrator creates your user account, he gives you a name (your user name) and assigns a password. The administrator does some other stuff, too—like specifying how often you're supposed to change your password, setting the hours you can log on, and so on. We'll talk about some of this a little later in the chapter.

If you're running NT on just a single computer that isn't connected to any network, somebody still needs to create user accounts for that single computer. Mechanically, the process works the same way—except that the user accounts only exist and only work on that one machine. And, oh yeah, there's probably one other difference, too. If you are working on a single, stand-alone machine, a network administrator may not be around to do or help you do all this stuff. You may have to do it yourself.

On most networks, a special computer called a *domain controller* does the work of authenticating computer accounts and user accounts. To return to our country club analogy introduced earlier, domain controllers work like those little guardhouses you see near the entrance to a really nice country club. There, a guard in uniform checks your name against the membership directory. On a network, a domain controller checks your computer's name and your name against the computer and user directory.

Okay, that's really all you need to understand about accounts. There's lots more I could say. But you don't really need to understand any more about the inner workings of account authentication to work with NT. So let's move on to rights.

A computer network might consist of multiple domains, which is why you need to specify which domain you're logging on to when your computer connects to a network. If your computer doesn't connect to a network, you log on to your computer—not the domain.

Rights Amount to Special Privileges

Here's the next thing you need to understand: not all accounts are created equal. Some accounts (like those of administrators) can do just about anything they want. Other accounts (like those of guests) don't get to do squat, really. These differences primarily stem from the differences in the "rights" accorded to different users. This sounds really complicated—or at least it does if you read the NT documentation. But all it really means is this: NT controls which actions a user can perform, such as accessing a particular computer from the network, backing up files, changing the system time, and so forth. For the most part, then, what rights really amount to is the ability of some user to start and run a particular program (like the NT Backup program) or to choose a command (like the Start menu's Shut Down command).

Permissions Control Access to Specific Resources

Permissions specify what you can and can't do with a disk, folder, file, or printer (NT calls these items *resources*). When you tell NT, for example, that you want to open a file, it makes sure that you have permission to do so. When you tell NT that you want to save a file, it again makes sure that you have permission to do so.

Groups Simplify the Poor Administrator's Workload

Now that you understand what rights and permissions are, you'll find it really easy to understand what groups are. Groups amount to predefined sets of rights and permissions. In other words, you don't have to individually specify every right and permission that some new user has. You can create a group with a predefined set of rights and permissions for, say, everybody in accounting. Then, the next time you add a new accounting department user, you can just say, "Oh, George? Well, he's in accounting so he should have all of the accounting group's rights and permissions."

Audit Logs Monitor Your Work

There's one final security tool I want to mention—just so you'll know about it. NT also lets you monitor, or audit, what users do. You can, for example, monitor when people are logging on to and off of the network. You can check to see whether people are trying to open particular files (perhaps those in your personal documents folder). You can see whether people are attempting to use rights they don't actually possess.

CAUTION

Rights override permissions. For example, if you have a super-secret business plan, you can specify that no one has permission to read the file. People with the "backup files and directories" right, however, can still read the file because they need to be able to do so in order to back it up.

WORKING WITH ACCOUNTS AND GROUPS

For purposes of this discussion, I assume you're creating an account for a stand-alone computer and not for a domain. Creating a domain account, however, works the same basic way as I describe here.

Once you understand what accounts are and why NT uses them, you'll have no trouble setting them up—assuming you have the right "right." Log on as the administrator, click the Start button, and then choose Programs | Administrative Tools | User Manager. NT displays the User Manager program window, as shown in Figure 6.1.

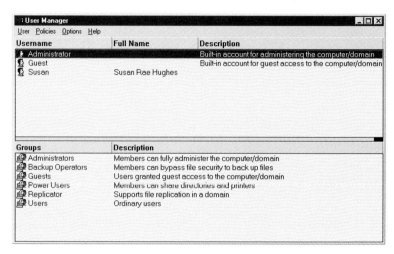

Figure 6.1 You use the User Manager to create accounts

habits & strategies

Don't do all your computing logged on as the administrator. With your unlimited authority you might inadvertently do all sorts of bad stuff, such as introduce a virus (which might then do anything to your machine since you, the administrator, "started" the program) or overwrite some important file.

Because you're perhaps seeing the User Manager program window for the first time, let me just point out one or two things. First of all, notice that in the top half of the program window, NT displays a list of the existing accounts. When you install NT, it automatically creates two accounts: an Administrator account, which has full rights and permission to do everything, and a guest account, which has very limited rights and is initially disabled.

In the bottom half of the program window, NT displays a list of existing groups. (Remember that, basically, a group is just a set of predefined rights and permissions.) When you install NT on a stand-alone computer (a workstation), it automatically creates the groups shown in Figure 6.1. I could create some massive table explaining what's different about the various groups. But, really, the descriptions that you see in the window are pretty accurate generalizations. Administrator accounts, for example, are for administrators. User accounts are for regular users. The other accounts that fall between these two extremes are for users whose abilities or responsibilities fall between those of an administrator or of a user.

Creating a New Account

To create a new user account, choose the User | New User command. NT displays the New User dialog box (see Figure 6.2). You provide the user name (this is the name that NT will use to identify the user to the network or to the stand-alone computer), the full name, and a password. You type the password twice just to confirm that you really know what you're entering. (To hide your password from spying eyes, NT displays asterisks in place of characters you type.)

You're an observant reader, of course, so you've noticed those check boxes at the bottom of the dialog box: User Must Change Password at Next Logon, User Cannot Change Password, Password Never Expires, and Account Disabled. These work just the way you expect. If you want the user to change his or her password at the next

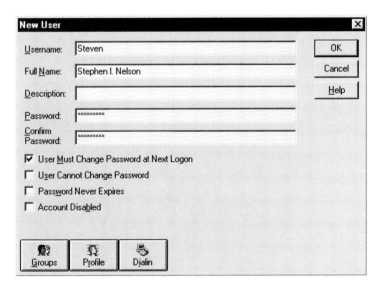

Figure 6.2 You use the New User dialog box to identify a new user and specify a password

logon, for example, you mark the User Must Change Password at Next Logon check box. If for some reason you have a question about one of these check boxes, click the Help button and read what Help has to say about these settings.

Near the bottom of the New User dialog box, you see three command buttons: Groups, Profile, and Dialin. The most important of these command buttons is Groups. When you click it, NT displays another dialog box that lets you specify which groups this new account is a member of: Administrators, Backup Operators, Guests, Power Users, or Users. You can also specify that the new account is a member of multiple groups if you want a user to have rights or permissions from more than a single group.

I wouldn't worry about the Profile or Dialin command buttons. The Profile command button just tells NT to display a dialog box that you can use to specify, basically, what happens when users log on to the computer or network and where NT suggests they store their stuff. The Dialin command button specifies how the users' accounts work when they use NT's remote access service, or RAS. User profiles and RAS are neat, no doubt, but if you're not an administrator, they're probably more than you want to get into.

Editing an Existing Account

If you want to edit some element of an existing account—change the password, for example—start the User Manager program as described earlier (log on as the administrator, click the Start button, and then choose Programs | Administrative Tools | User Manager). Then double-click the user's account. NT displays the User Properties dialog box, which mirrors the New User dialog box shown in Figure 6.2. You make your changes and click OK.

If you want to permanently delete an account, start the User Manager program, click the user account (to select it), and then choose the User | Delete command.

Creating a New Group

You aren't limited to using the groups that NT automatically creates when it installs itself. You can create new groups, too. And this

habits & strategies

If there's even the slightest chance you may want to later reuse an account, you should disable rather than delete the account by marking the Account Disabled check box. For all but the largest NT networks, there's no practical limit on the number of user accounts you can have.

is a pretty good idea whenever you've got a group of users who need the same rights or the same permissions. All of the people in a payroll accounting department, for example, probably need access to the same confidential payroll information files. So if you actually encountered this situation in real life, you would probably want to create a group that describes whatever special rights the payroll department needs and the permissions needed to work with the payroll files.

To create a new group (called a *local group* for reasons we don't go into here), start the User Manager as described earlier. Select the users you want to add to the new group. You can select multiple users by holding down the CTRL key and then individually clicking each user. Then choose the User | New Local Group command. When NT displays the New Local Group dialog box (see Figure 6.3), name and describe the group. Then click OK.

If you're setting up the local group on a stand-alone computer, but you're connected to a network, you can click the Add button to display a dialog box that lists network users.

Editing an Existing Group

If you want to edit an existing group's name or description, start the User Manager program as described earlier. Then double-click the group. NT displays the Local Group Properties dialog box, which mirrors

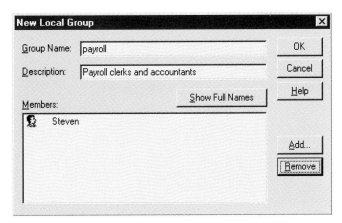

Figure 6.3 The New Local Group dialog box lets you name and describe a new group of users

the New Local Group dialog box shown in Figure 6.3. You make your changes and click OK.

Specifying Account Policies

Let me mention one other aspect of the account security tool. NT lets you specify certain policies or general rules, for your accounts (mostly having to do with how passwords are created). By default, these rules are very loose. If you're serious about your computer's or network's security, therefore, you'll want to tighten up NT's account policies.

To set overall account policy for all of the accounts on a computer or network, start the User Manager as described earlier. Then choose the Policies | Account command. When NT displays the Account Policy dialog box (see Figure 6.4), use it to describe how passwords should

CAUTION

NT's initial account policy settings are pretty loosey-goosey.

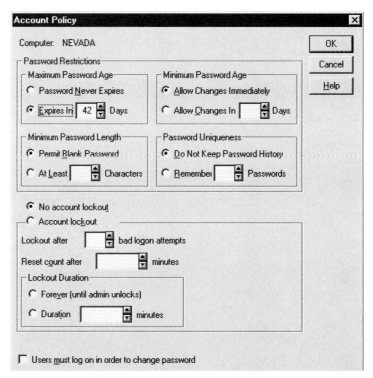

Figure 6.4 The boxes and buttons that appear on the Account Policy dialog box are all pretty self-explanatory, but you can click the Help button if you have questions

be created and updated as well as what happens when someone tries to log on, like, 47 times in a row without success. I'm not going to describe here how each of the individual boxes and buttons on the Account Policy dialog box work. For one thing, most of them are obvious. For another, you can get good descriptions of what each box and button does by clicking the Help command button.

WORKING WITH RIGHTS

Working with rights isn't difficult. You simply assign rights to groups (and optionally, to individual user accounts). Let me quickly explain how this works. You start the User Manager, as described earlier. Next, you choose the Policies | User Rights command so that NT displays the User Rights Policy dialog box (see Figure 6.5). In this dialog box, activate the Right drop-down list box and select the right you want to assign to a group. Once you do this, NT displays a list of the groups that already have this right. If you want to add a group, click the Add button so that NT displays a list of groups and users (see Figure 6.6).

Use the List Names From dialog box to indicate whether you want to see network user accounts and groups or stand-alone computer user accounts and groups. Once NT provides the appropriate list of users and groups, add users and groups to the list of users and groups that have the right by double-clicking. (This reads funny, but remember that

habits & strategies

It's unlikely that you'll want to assign some right you don't understand, but you can click the Help button to display a window of information that includes a clickable hyperlink to a painfully detailed description of each of the user rights.

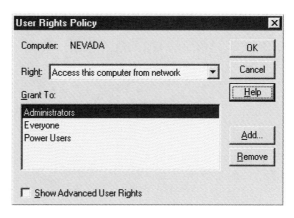

Figure 6.5 The User Rights Policy dialog box lets you specify what users and groups can do

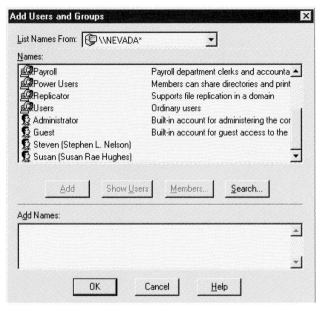

Figure 6.6 The Add Users and Groups dialog box lets you identify the new user or group that should have a particular right

what you're doing is adding users or groups to the list of people who already have the selected right.) When you finish, click OK.

If you want to remove a user or group from the list of users and groups that have the selected right, choose the Policies | User Rights command so that NT displays the User Rights Policy dialog box shown in Figure 6.5. Using the Right drop-down list box, select the right you want to withdraw from a particular user or group. Click the user or group to select it. Then click the Remove command button.

WORKING WITH PERMISSIONS

Permissions specify what you can and can't do with network resources such as disks, folders, files, and printers. Setting permissions for printers is easy, so I'll save that for last. Setting permissions for disks, folders, and files is more complicated (at least more complicated to explain), because permissions work differently depending on your file system.

Appendix A talks about the whole FAT vs. NTFS debate in a bit more detail.

habits & strategies

You can also set share permissions for NTFS disks, but share permissions aren't really necessary or useful because you can instead set regular, resource-level permissions.

Chapter 3 describes how you start and work with My Computer.

Your file system determines how the operating system keeps track of the files you store on your hard disk. NT 4.0 supports two file systems: FAT (which is really the old MS-DOS file system) and NTFS (which is NT's slick and secure file system).

Setting Share Permissions on a FAT Disk

If a particular disk's file system is FAT, you can't really control access to a disk's files. You can, however, control network access to the disk by setting share permissions. Or, restated another way, share permissions don't control all access to a disk, but they do control network access to a disk. That sounds illogical, so let me explain. By setting a share permission, you tell NT that network users can't grab stuff from, say, your hard disk drive C. If you do this, NT does protect your disk from network users. However, because your disk's file system is FAT (which is a crummy old file system if ever there was one), you can't prevent someone from booting your computer using, say, MS-DOS, and then using MS-DOS to muck about on your hard disk.

To set the share permissions on a FAT disk drive, start My Computer and right-click the disk you want to set share permissions for. NT displays the shortcut menu for that disk. Choose the Sharing command from the shortcut menu so that NT displays the Properties dialog box with the Sharing tab showing (see Figure 6.7).

You'll need to first share the disk before you can set share permissions. If you haven't already done this, mark the Shared As option button to indicate that this disk should be shared and then accept the suggested share name, which will be the drive letter or folder name. (If you're sharing a root directory, you'll need to click the New Share button and then Permissions.)

Next, click the Permissions command button so that NT displays the Access Through Share Permissions dialog box (see Figure 6.8). Use the Type of Access drop-down list box to specify what people can do with the shared disk's information:

- Full Control (people can do anything they want)
- No Access (people can't do anything)

- Read (people can open and view files stored on the disk)
- Change (people can open, view, and update files stored on the disk)

If you want to specify different permissions for different users or groups, you can do that, too. First, in the Access Through Share Permissions dialog box (Figure 6.8), select the Everyone group and specify everyone's Type of Access as Full Control. Then click the Add command button so that NT displays the Add Users and Groups dialog box (see Figure 6.9).

In the Add Users and Groups dialog box, use the List Names From drop-down list box to indicate whether you want to see your computer's user accounts and groups or the network's user accounts and groups. When NT lists the accounts and groups you want, double-click those you want to add. Then use the Type of Access drop-down list box to specify what permissions the selected account or group should have. After you do this, click the OK button.

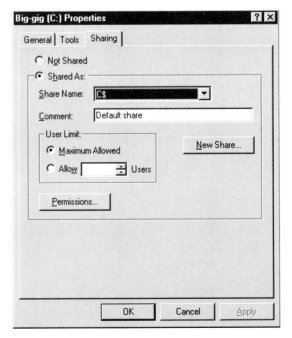

Figure 6.7 You use the Properties dialog box when you want to share and set share permissions for a FAT disk

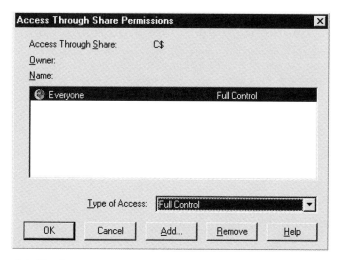

Figure 6.8 The Access Through Share Permissions dialog box lets you set share permissions

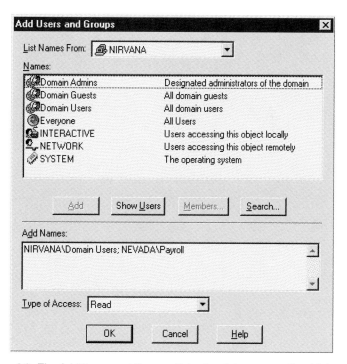

Figure 6.9 The Add Users and Groups dialog box lets you specify which users and groups you want to set share permissions for

Now you're back in the Access Through Share Permissions dialog box. Click OK to close this dialog box. Click OK again to close the Properties dialog box.

Setting Permissions on an NTFS Disk

If a particular disk's file system is NTFS, you can control access to each and every folder and file on a disk using either user accounts or groups, as long as you're the owner of the folder or file. To be considered the owner, either you created the folder or file (the usual case) or you were assigned ownership of the folder or file by the previous owner (probably the administrator).

To set the permissions on an NTFS disk drive, start My Computer and then display the disk, folder, or file you want to set permissions for. Right-click the item so that NT displays the shortcut menu. Select Properties, and when NT displays the Normal Properties dialog box, click the Security tab (see Figure 6.10).

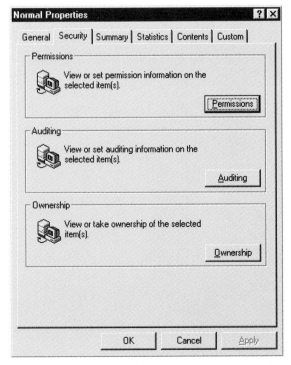

Figure 6.10 You use the Security tab in the Normal Properties dialog box to set permissions for an NTFS disk

Next, click the Permissions command button so that NT displays the File Permissions dialog box as shown in Figure 6.11 (or another dialog box similar to this one, depending on whether you've selected a file, a folder, or a disk).

In the File Permissions dialog box, use the Type of Access drop-down list box to specify what people can do with the shared disk's information: Full Control, No Access, Read, and Change.

To specify different permissions for different users or groups, first select the Everyone group shown in the File Permissions dialog box and specify everyone's Type of Access as Full Control. Then, add users or groups to the list box shown in Figure 6.11 by clicking the Add command button so that NT displays the Add Users and Groups dialog box (see Figure 6.12). Use the List Names From drop-down list box to indicate whether you want to see your computer's user accounts and groups or the network's user accounts and groups. When NT lists the accounts and groups you want, double-click the one you want to set file permissions for. Then use the Type of Access dialog box to specify what permissions the selected account or group should have.

After you finish specifying which user accounts and groups you want to set file permissions for, click the OK button to return to the File

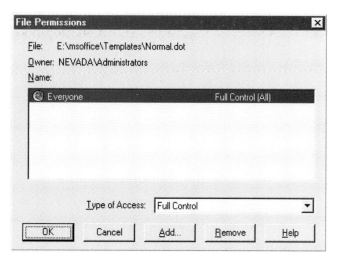

Figure 6.11 The File Permissions dialog box lets you set permissions for an individual file

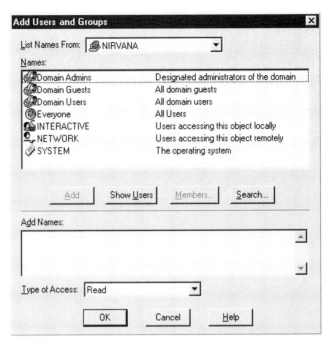

Figure 6.12 The Add Users and Groups dialog box lets you specify which users and groups you want to set file permissions for

Permissions dialog box. Click OK to close the File Permissions dialog box. Click OK to close the Properties dialog box.

Setting Permissions on a Printer

You can also set permissions on a local printer, too, as long as you're the owner (this really means that you're the one who installed the printer). This works very much the same as setting share permissions for a directory, so I'll just describe the process in very abbreviated detail. You start My Computer and open the Printers folder so that the printer's shortcut icon shows. You right-click the printer so its shortcut menu shows, and then you select the Sharing command. When NT displays the printer's Properties dialog box (see Figure 6.13), you mark the Shared option button and provide a name for the now-shared printer using the Share Name text box.

To exercise more control over the way your printer is shared, click the Security tab of the printer's Properties dialog box. Next, click the

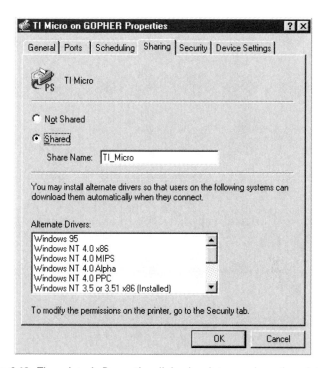

Figure 6.13 The printer's Properties dialog box lets you share the printer

Permissions command button so that NT displays the Printer Permissions dialog box (see Figure 6.14).

To specify what printer permissions a selected user or group should have, select the user or group. Then, use the Type of Access drop-down list box to specify what the user or group can do with the printer: Full Control (the user or group can do anything with the printer), No Access (the user or group can't use the printer), Print (the user or group can print stuff but do nothing else), and Manage Documents (the user or groups can noodle around with the spool files in the print queue, as described in Chapter 5).

To specify different permissions for different users or groups than those shown, add users or groups to the list box by clicking the Add command button so that NT displays the Add Users and Groups dialog box (I'm not going to show this dialog box, since it's the same one you've seen earlier in this section on permissions). Use the List Names

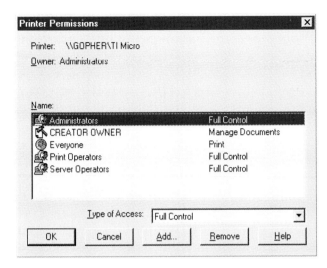

Figure 6.14 The Printer Permissions dialog box lets you set permissions for an individual printer

From drop-down list box to indicate whether you want to see your computer's user accounts and groups or the network's user accounts and groups. When NT lists the accounts and groups you want, double-click the one you want to set printer permissions for. Then use the Type of Access dialog box to specify what printer permissions the selected account or group should have.

After you finish specifying which user accounts and groups you want to set printer permissions for, click the OK button to return to the Printer Permissions dialog box. Click OK to close the Printer Permissions dialog box. Click OK to close the printer's Properties dialog box.

WORKING WITH AUDIT LOGS

Audit logs, which represent NT's final security tool, track changes that users make to a resource, including changes to the resource's permissions and ownership.

To create an audit log, start My Computer and then display the resource you want to audit. (Remember that a resource can be a disk, folder, file, or printer.) Right-click the item so that NT displays the shortcut menu. Select Properties, and when NT displays the Properties dialog box, click the Security tab (see Figure 6.15).

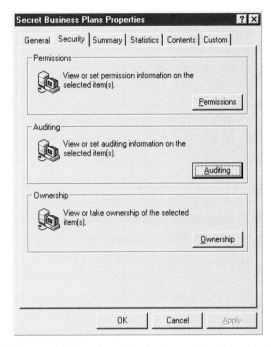

habits & strategies

The Ownership command button, which also appears on the Properties dialog box shown in Figure 6.15, lets you view the ownership of a resource and lets some users (like administrators) take over the ownership of the selected item so he or she can set permissions for the item. Typically, the owner of a resource is the person who created the resource.

Figure 6.15 You use the Security tab in the Properties dialog box to turn on auditing of a resource

Next, click the Auditing command button so that NT displays the File Auditing dialog box (see Figure 6.16), or another dialog box similar to this one, depending on whether you've selected a file, a folder, a printer, and so on.

Click the Add command button to display the Add Users and Groups dialog box. Then use the List Names From drop-down list box to indicate whether you want to see your computer's user accounts and groups or the network's user accounts and groups. When NT lists the accounts and groups you want, double-click the one you want to audit. Or just double-click the special Everyone group if you want to audit every user's activities with regard to the selected item. Click OK to return to the File Auditing dialog box. Then use its check boxes to specify what activities you want reported in the audit log for this item. Most of the check boxes describe activities that are self-explanatory, but if you have questions, remember that you can just click the Help command button.

To view the audit log, you use the Event Viewer program, which is described in Chapter 8.

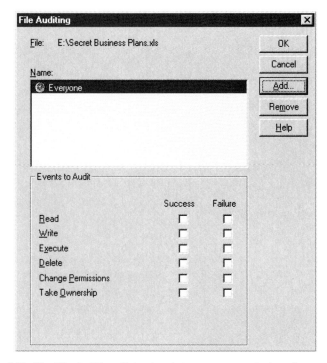

Figure 6.16 The File Auditing dialog box lets you set permissions for an individual file

ON FROM HERE

With the information provided in this chapter, you now understand the essential nuts and bolts of working with NT. For this reason, much of the material that's covered in subsequent chapters isn't essential for using NT. Nevertheless, consider taking a peek at Chapter 7, since it describes how you work with many of the popular and useful Control Panel tools. And, if you've got time, take a peek at Chapter 8, too. It describes some powerful utilities as well as some of the neat accessories and add-on programs that come free with NT.

CHAPTER 7

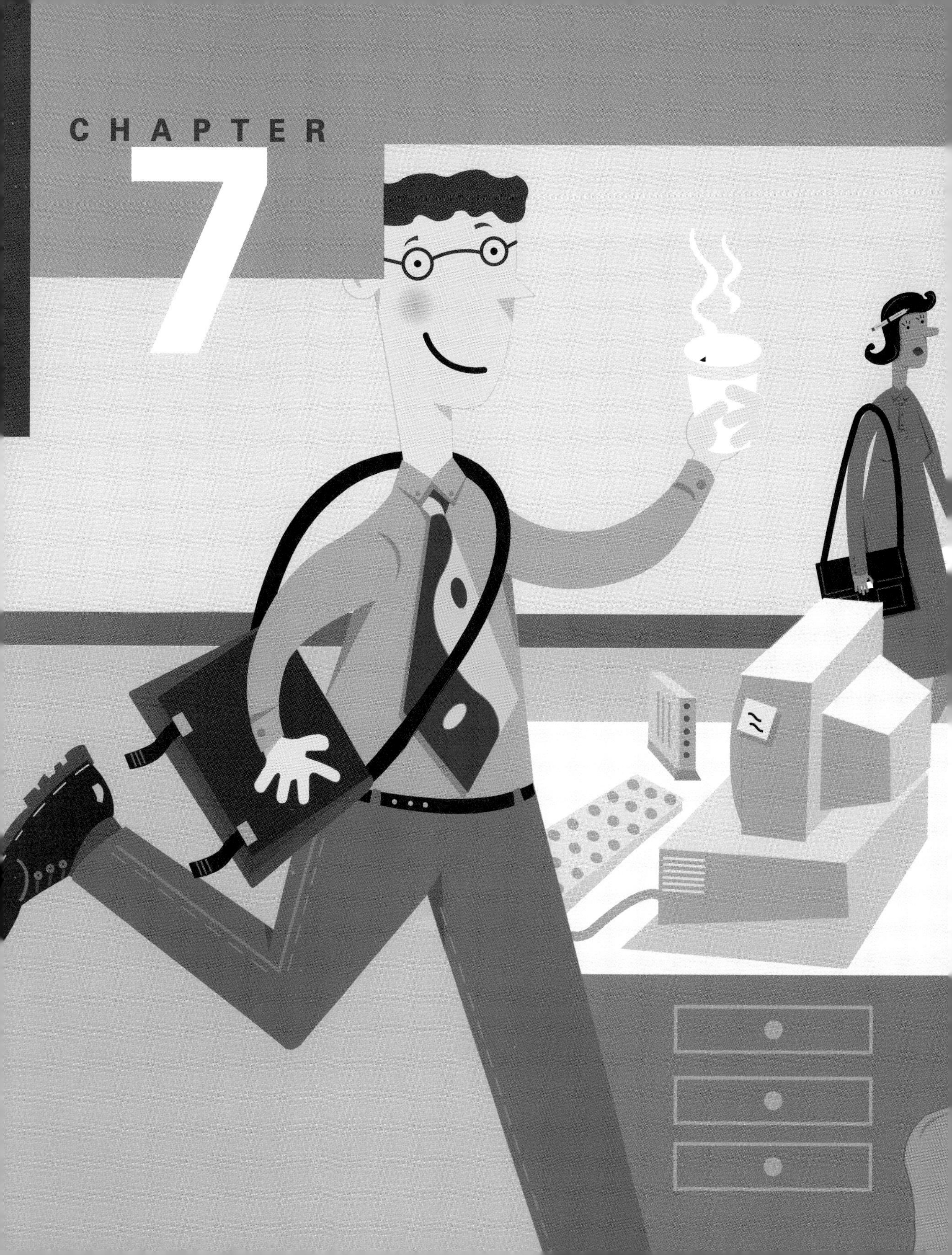

Handy NT Accessories

INCLUDES

- Using Calculator

- Using Paint

- Using Phone Dialer

- Using WordPad

FAST FORWARD

START CALCULATOR ➤ *p. 118*
To start Calculator, click Start. Then choose Programs | Accessories | Calculator. When NT displays the Calculator, click its value and operator keys to perform your calculations. If you want to make statistical, mathematical, or trigonometric calculations, choose the View | Scientific command so you can use the more powerful scientific version of the NT Calculator.

START PAINT ➤ *p. 123*
To start Paint, click Start. Then choose the Programs | Accessories | Paint command. When NT displays the Paint program window, click a color box to select the color you want to draw in. Then click the drawing tool you want to use. To use a drawing tool, click or drag a mouse in the Paint drawing area.

**SAVE, OPEN, AND PRINT
IMAGES IN PAINT** ➤ *p. 127*
To save a Paint image you've created, choose the File | Save command. To later open an image you've previously saved, choose the File | Open command. To print an image, choose the File | Print command.

START PHONE DIALER ➤ *p. 128*
To start Phone Dialer, click Start. Then choose the Programs | Accessories | Phone Dialer command. When NT displays the Phone Dialer program window, click the unprogrammed speed dial buttons to program names and numbers. To dial a number once you've set it up, click the appropriate speed dial button.

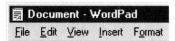

START WORDPAD ➤ *p. 130*

To start WordPad, click Start. Then choose the Programs |
Accessories | WordPad command. When NT displays the WordPad
program window, create your document by typing.

[<u>O</u>pen]

SAVE, OPEN, AND PRINT
WORDPAD DOCUMENTS ➤ *p. 132*

To save a WordPad document, choose the File | Save command. To
open a WordPad document, choose the File | Open command. To
print a WordPad document, choose the File | Print command.

When you install NT, you don't just get the operating system. You also get a bunch of other programs as well. Most of these other accessory programs—NT calls most of them *accessories*—are worth just what you pay for them (nothing). But a handful of them really are useful. So I want to quickly describe four of the best accessories here: Calculator, Paint, Phone Dialer, and WordPad.

USING CALCULATOR

Perhaps because I'm an accountant by training, I think NT's slick little Calculator program is its handiest accessory (WordPad, which I describe last in this chapter, runs a close second). It's not that Calculator does anything particularly unique. It works like one of those handheld calculators that you might still have in the drawer of your desk. The thing that's handy about Calculator is that it's darn convenient. It's always just a click or two away.

Calculator Basics

To start Calculator, click Start. Then choose Programs | Accessories | Calculator. NT displays the Calculator shown in Figure 7.1.

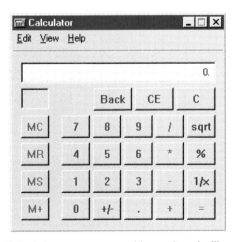

Figure 7.1 The Calculator program resembles and works like a handheld calculator

To use the calculator, click its value and operator keys. For example, to add the values 2 and 2, click the following keys:

```
2 + 2 =
```

When you do, Calculator displays the result 4.

Other calculations work in an equally predictable manner. To subtract the value 5 from the value 10, click the following keys:

```
10 - 5 =
```

To multiply the value 5 by the value 25, click these keys:

```
5 * 25 =
```

To divide the value 100 by 14, click these keys:

```
100 / 14 =
```

To calculate the square root of the value 10000, click these keys:

```
10000 sqrt
```

To calculate what value is 25% of the value 400, click these keys:

```
400 * 25 %
```

To calculate the reciprocal of the value 2, click these keys:

```
2 1/x
```

If you want to change the sign of the value 45 (from positive to negative), click these keys:

```
45 +/-
```

Calculator supplies a handful of other keys to make your calculations easier. Here's the Clear Entry key:

It erases the last value you entered. Or, restated slightly different, the Clear Entry key erases whatever number keys you've clicked since you clicked the last mathematical operator key.

Here's the Back key:

Use the Calculator's period key when you need to indicate a decimal point in a value such as 1.234.

To calculate the reciprocal of a value, Calculator divides 1 by the value. For example, the reciprocal of the value 2 equals 1/2, or .5. The reciprocal of a reciprocal equals the original value. For example, the reciprocal of .5 equals 2.

It erases the last number key you clicked. For example, if you have just entered the value 12345, then clicking Back once erases the 5. Clicking Back twice erases the 5 and 4. Clicking Back three times...you get the picture, right?

Here's the Clear key:

It erases the value shown on the calculator display. You click Clear when you want to erase everything you've already done and start over.

Calculator provides a memory function similar to that of many handheld calculators. Here's the Memory Store key:

If you click it, Calculator stores the value currently shown in the calculator display. Calculator can only store one value at a time in memory, so when you click Memory Store to store a new value, you replace the old value. To indicate that a value is stored in memory, Calculator displays the letter M in the small gray box above the row of Memory buttons.

To retrieve a value from memory so you can use it in a calculation, click the Memory Recall key, shown here:

Once you retrieve a value from memory using the Memory Recall key, of course, you use it in a calculation.

You can also click the Memory Add key:

Clicking this key adds the displayed value to whatever value is already stored in memory and to then store this calculation result in memory.

To erase the value stored in memory, click the Memory Clear key:

This all makes perfect sense, right? You've used a calculator before. You know how to click keys.

Moving Values from and to the Calculator

You can copy the value shown on the calculator display to the NT Clipboard. The Clipboard is a temporary storage area that lets you copy and move information within a program (such as your word processor) and between programs (such as from Calculator to an accounting program). To copy the value shown on the calculator display to the Clipboard, choose the Edit | Copy command. To copy the value stored in the Clipboard to the calculator display—this action is equivalent to entering the value using the Calculator keypad—choose the Edit | Paste command.

I don't want to sound like a kid who's excited about a new toy, but this ability of using the Clipboard to move calculation results from and to different programs is really useful. If you want to quickly make a calculation for a report and then use that value in the report, the Calculator comes to your aid. Start the Calculator. Make the calculation. Choose the Edit | Copy command. Switch back to the program where you want to copy the value, such as by clicking the other program's task bar button. And then choose that program's Edit | Paste command.

Using the Scientific View of the Calculator

The version of the Calculator program window shown in Figure 7.1 lets you make simple calculations. But you can't do anything really tricky. Does this mean you can't use Calculator for more complicated formulas? Not at all. If you choose the View | Scientific command, the Calculator program window changes to what's shown in Figure 7.2.

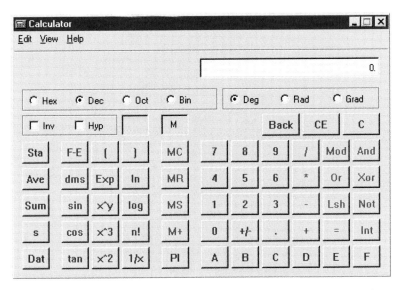

Figure 7.2 The scientific view of the Calculator lets you make more complex calculations

The Calculator's scientific view provides almost all the same buttons that the simpler standard view does. It also provides a bunch of other buttons for performing statistical, mathematical, and trigonometric calculations. For example, if you want to calculate the sine of the value 0, click these keys:

```
0 sin
```

To calculate the cosine of the value 0, click these keys:

```
0 cos
```

The scientific view of the NT calculator does way more than I can explain in a few paragraphs. (In fact, I think someone could probably write an entire book about the program, providing good, detailed information on the hows and whys of its various statistical and trigonometric calculations.) Nevertheless, if you're familiar with the overall logic of a particular calculation, you should find it pretty easy to figure out how to use the Calculator to perform it. If you're not clear about the function of a particular Calculator key—say it's the Sum key—just right-click on the key. NT displays the following What's This? command button:

| What's This? |

Click the What's This? button to display a pop-up box of helpful information about how to use the Sum key:

> Calculates the sum of the values displayed in the **Statistics** box. To calculate the sum of the squares, use Inv+Sum.
>
> This button is available only if you click **Sta** first.
>
> Keyboard equivalent = CTRL+T

The one tricky thing to figure out is how you make statistical calculations with the scientific view of the calculator. So here's a brief explanation of how this works. First, click the Sta key to open the Statistics box, which Calculator uses to store the values you'll analyze. Next, collect the values you want to analyze by clicking the Calculator keypad keys (to describe the value) and then add to the Statistics box by clicking the Dat key. Once you collect all of the values, use the Sum, Ave, and s keys to calculate the sum, average, and standard deviation of the values stored in the Statistics box.

USING PAINT

The Paint accessory lets you create simple bitmap images. Like the kind a small child might draw (see Figure 7.3). No, you're not going to create great art with Paint. But you know what? You can actually do some pretty fun stuff: quick-and-dirty drawings, simple-yet-colorful illustrations, and so forth.

Painting Basics

To start Paint, click Start. Then choose the Programs | Accessories | Paint command. NT displays the Paint program window. Initially, the Paint program window shows an empty, or blank, page because you haven't yet begun drawing.

Figure 7.3 My 5-year-old daughter drew this picture—apparently of me—using Paint

To draw a line or shape, first click a color box. The color boxes appear at the bottom of the program window. Then click the drawing tool you want to use; the tool box appears along the left side of the program window. Then click and drag the mouse inside the drawing area. Figure 7.4 shows the lines or shapes that each of the drawing tools creates. Starting at the top, you see a pencil-drawn line, a brush stroke, an airbrush spray, text in a text box, a straight line, a curved line, a rectangle, a polygon, and then along the bottom edge an ellipse and a rectangle with rounded corners. Notice that the long-suffering desktop publisher who laid out this page placed pictures of the Paint tool used with each drawing object in the margin and then drew arrows from the tool images to the drawing objects.

You can use the Magnifier tool—it's the one that looks like a magnifying glass on the tool box—to zoom in or out of the Paint image. To do this, click the Magnifying tool; then select the zoom factor you want (these show up in a list beneath the drawing tools).

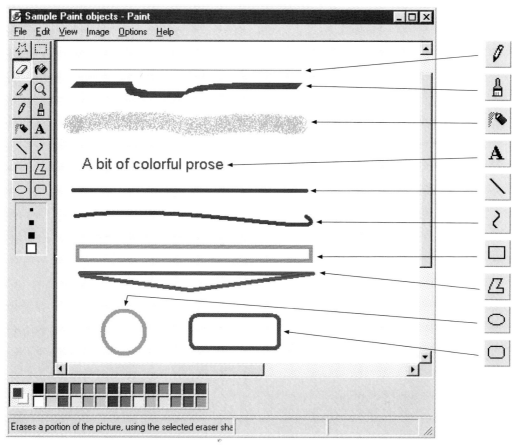

Figure 7.4 Sure, this Figure ain't great art, but it does show which tools create which drawing objects

You can use the Pick Color tool—it's the one that looks like an eyedropper on the tool box—to change the selected color box to an existing color. To do this, first click the Pick Color tool. Then click a drawing object (inside the Paint drawing area) that uses the color to select, or pick, that color. You can use the Fill with Color tool—it's the one that looks like a paint can pouring paint on the tool box—to fill an area with a specified color. To do this, click the Fill with Color tool, click the color box, and then click the area you want to fill.

Editing Images

Image editing works a bit differently in Paint (as compared to other programs). Basically, you use three tools from the tool box in your editing: the Free-Form Select tool, the Select tool, and the Eraser tool.

The Free-Form Select tool lets you select a polygon-shaped image area so it can be copied or moved. To use the Free-Form Select tool, first select the tool by clicking it:

Then select the image area you want to cut or copy by dragging the mouse along the image area's border. This sounds tricky, but try it on an image that doesn't matter. You'll quickly see how it works. Next, choose the Edit | Cut command to move the image area you've selected to the Clipboard. Or choose the Edit | Copy command to move a copy of the image area you've selected to the Clipboard. To move the cut or copied image area from the Clipboard to a new location, choose the Edit | Paste command.

The Select tool lets you select a rectangular image area so it can be copied or moved. To use the Select tool, select the tool by clicking it:

Then select the rectangle you want to cut or copy by dragging the mouse between the rectangle's two opposite corners. Next, choose the Edit | Cut command to move the image area you've selected to the Clipboard. Or choose the Edit | Copy command to move a copy of the image area you've selected to the Clipboard. To paste the cut or copied image area from the Clipboard, choose the Edit | Paste command.

The Eraser tool erases portions of an image. To use the Eraser tool, select the tool by clicking it:

Select the size of the eraser head from the list box that Paint displays beneath the drawing tools (Paint doesn't display this list box until you click the Eraser tool). Next, erase portions of the image by dragging the mouse.

Saving, Opening, and Printing Images

When saving Paint images, later opening these images, and printing images, Paint works like other NT programs. To save the image you've created, choose the File | Save command. If you haven't saved the image before, Paint displays the Save As dialog box (see Figure 7.5), which you use to name the image and specify where you want it saved. If you've worked much with the My Computer program, you'll have no trouble using the Save As dialog box. Think of it as My Computer run through a really hot wash cycle and then shrunk in the dryer.

habits & strategies

If you're not all that familiar with My Computer, know that you can use the Save in drop-down list to specify the disk and folder you want to use for saving the image and that you use the File name box to name your image.

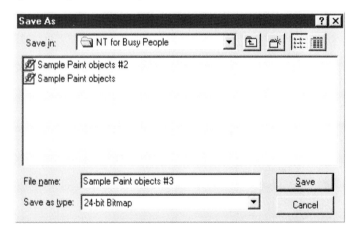

Figure 7.5 The Save As dialog box lets you specify where a file should be saved and what name should be used for the file

To later open an image you've previously saved—perhaps so you can admire your handiwork—choose the File | Open command. When Paint displays the Open dialog box (see Figure 7.6), use the Look in drop-down list box to provide the file's location and the File name text box to give the file's names. If you see the file listed in the Open dialog box, you can also just double-click the file to open it.

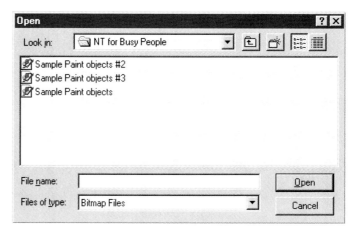

Figure 7.6 The Open dialog box lets you find a file you want to open

Chapter 5 describes in detail how printing works with NT. Refer to that chapter if you have questions about how to print with any NT program or accessory.

Printing? You won't have any trouble with this. Just choose the File | Print command. When Paint displays the Print dialog box, give any additional instructions to Paint (such as the number of copies you want printed). Then click OK.

USING PHONE DIALER

Phone Dialer is a funny little thing. It keeps a small database of frequently called telephone numbers. As long as your modem connects to the same telephone line as your telephone, you can use Phone Dialer to in effect pick up the phone and dial the specified number. As kooky as this might sound, it works pretty well.

To start Phone Dialer, click Start. Then choose the Programs | Accessories | Phone Dialer command. NT displays the Phone Dialer program window (see Figure 7.7).

There are a couple of ways to use Phone Dialer. The "it really isn't worth the effort" way is to enter a telephone number into the Number to dial text box (you can either type the telephone number using the keyboard or click the telephone numbers on the program's keypad). Then click the Dial command button. This works. But it isn't pretty.

The right way to use Phone Dialer is to store speed dial numbers you'll want to dial again and again. To do this, click one of the Speed

Figure 7.7 The Phone Dialer program lets your (keyboard) fingers do the dialing

dial buttons that appear along the right edge of the Phone Dialer program window. Phone Dialer displays the Program Speed Dial dialog box:

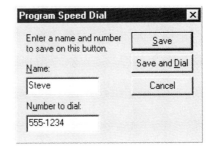

Enter the name of the person or business in the Name text box. Garth. Peter. Joanne, or whatever. Then use the Number to dial text box to provide the telephone number you want Phone Dialer to dial. When you finish providing the name and number, click the Save button if you just want to save the speed dial number. Or, click the Save and Dial button to both save the speed dial number and dial it.

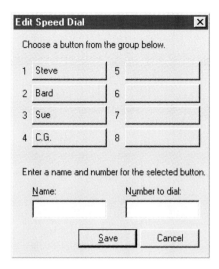

Figure 7.8 The Edit Speed Dial dialog box lets you edit existing speed dial numbers

To use a speed dial number once you've programmed it, you just click the appropriate speed dial button.

If you later want to change a speed dial number, choose the Edit | Speed Dial command. Then, when Phone Dialer displays the Edit Speed Dial dialog box (see Figure 7.8), click the speed dial number you want to change and use the Name and Number to dial text boxes to make your changes.

USING WORDPAD

WordPad lets you create simple text documents. It's not anything fancy, I'll give you that. But it's free. It's easy to use. And it's smart about the sorts of documents it'll handle. With WordPad, for example, you can work with straight text files (files that contain no funny formatting information) or with Microsoft Word text files (files that contain lots of funny formatting information).

WordPad Basics

To start WordPad, click Start. Then choose the Programs | Accessories | WordPad command. NT displays the WordPad program window (see Figure 7.9). To create your WordPad document, just begin typing.

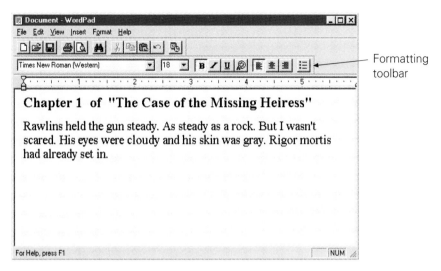

Formatting
toolbar

Figure 7.9   The WordPad program window shows the text document you're creating

You may be able to guess which formatting boxes and buttons are which. If you can't, however, just move the mouse pointer so it points to a box or button. WordPad displays the tool name in a small pop-up box. (This trick works with most program's toolbars, by the way.)

You can type anything you want—even bad pulp fiction. If you make a mistake, use the BACKSPACE key to erase the last character or characters you've typed.

You can add formatting to your WordPad document using the Formatting toolbar (it's the second toolbar shown in Figure 7.9). Use the Font box to specify the typeface you want to use for the selected text and the Point Size box to set size. Use the Bold, Italic, Underline, and Color buttons to bold, italicize, underline, and color the selected text. Use the Align Left, Center, and Align Right buttons to specify paragraph alignment for the selected text. Finally, use the Bullets button to turn each of the paragraphs in your text selection into bullet points.

Editing WordPad Documents

To insert new text in the middle of stuff you've already created, use the arrow keys to reposition the insertion point (the flashing bar). Then type the new material you want.

To replace existing text with something new, reposition the insertion point so it rests just ahead of the first character you want to replace, hold down the SHIFT key, and then use the right and down arrow keys to select, or highlight, the text you want to replace. For example, look at the following text:

In his other hand--the one that wasn't holding a gun--was a note. It started "Dear John." I didn't have to read the rest. I knew what it said.

You can also select text using the mouse. Click the first character you want to replace. Then drag the mouse to the last character you want to replace.

To replace the phrase "Dear John" with the phrase "Dear Peter," select the word "John" and then type "Peter." WordPad replaces "John" with "Peter."

In his other hand--the one that wasn't holding a gun--was a note. It started "Dear Peter." I didn't have to read the rest. I knew what it said.

WordPad lets you drag-and-drop text. If you're familiar with how this technique works in other applications, you already know how to drag-and-drop in WordPad. Use the mouse to select a block of text. Then drag the selection to move it to a new location. Or, hold down the CTRL key and drag the selection to copy it to a new location.

Saving, Opening, and Printing WordPad Documents

Saving, opening, and printing WordPad documents works like saving, opening, and printing Paint images. To save a document, choose the File | Save command. If you haven't saved the image before, WordPad displays the Save As dialog box (see Figure 7.5 earlier in the chapter), which you use to name the document and specify where you want it saved. As noted earlier in the Paint discussion, the Save As dialog box works very similarly to the My Computer program, so if you're familiar with the My Computer program you'll have no trouble using the Save As dialog box.

To later open a document, choose the File | Open command. Then, when WordPad displays the Open dialog box, use the Look in drop-down list box to locate the file and the File name text box to name the file.

To print a document, choose the File | Print command. When WordPad displays the Print dialog box (see Figure 7.10), use it to give any additional instructions to WordPad (such as the number of copies you want printed). Then click OK.

Chapter 5 describes in detail how printing works with NT. Refer to that chapter if you have questions about how to print with any NT program or accessory.

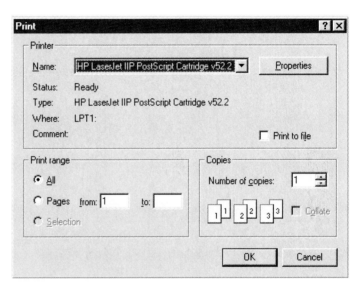

Figure 7.10 Use the Print dialog box to provide additional instructions to NT about how it should print the WordPad document

ON FROM HERE

The stuff covered in this chapter isn't very sophisticated. All we've talked about, really, are some easy-to-use yet very handy tools. So perhaps you've felt a bit underchallenged. Never fear, my friend. Chapter 8 describes in detail how to use some of the more powerful programs and tools that NT provides. If you'll continue your reading there, let me be the first to welcome you to the big leagues.

Power User Tools

INCLUDES

- Using Windows NT Explorer

- Using the command prompt

- Using Event Viewer

- Understanding Back Up, Disk Administrator, and Windows NT Diagnostics

FAST FORWARD

START NT EXPLORER ➤ *pp. 139-140*

Click the Start button. Then choose the Programs | Windows NT Explorer command. NT starts NT Explorer and displays its program window.

New Folder

CREATE NEW FOLDERS WITH NT EXPLORER ➤ *p. 142*

Start NT Explorer. Select the disk or folder to which you want to add the new folder. Choose the File | New | Folder command. NT Explorer adds a new, unnamed folder and opens an editable text box over the new folder's default name, "New Folder." Type the new folder name.

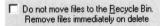

binder
cardfile
clipbrd
excel

OPEN FILES WITH NT EXPLORER ➤ *p. 143*

Start NT Explorer. Double-click the icon of the file you want to open. If you double-click a document icon, NT starts the program you used to create the document and then tells that program to open the file. If you open a program file, NT starts the program.

☐ Do not move files to the Recycle Bin.
  Remove files immediately on delete

DELETE AND UNDELETE FILES WITH NT EXPLORER ➤ *pp. 144-145*

Start NT Explorer. To delete a file, right-click it and then choose Delete. To undelete a file, open the Recycle Bin folder, right-click the file, and choose Restore.

My great American novel

RENAME FILES AND FOLDERS WITH NT EXPLORER ➤ *p. 145*

Start NT Explorer. Select the file and click the file name. Then, when NT Explorer opens a text box over the file name, type the new name you want to use for the file.

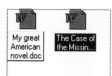

COPY AND MOVE FILES
WITH NT EXPLORER ➤ *p. 145*

Start NT Explorer. To move a file with NT Explorer, drag it from one folder to another folder. (You may need to expand more than one branch of the tree diagram shown in the folders pane before doing this.) To copy a file with NT Explorer, hold down the CTRL key and then drag it from one folder to another folder.

FORMAT FLOPPY DISKS
WITH NT EXPLORER ➤ *p. 146*

Start NT Explorer. Insert the floppy disk into the floppy disk drive. Right-click on the floppy disk icon to display its shortcut menu. Then choose the Format command.

331KB (Disk free space: 219MB)

MONITOR DISK SPACE
WITH NT EXPLORER ➤ *p. 146*

Start NT Explorer. Right-click the disk. Choose the Properties command from the shortcut menu. NT displays the disk's Properties dialog box, which uses a pie chart to show you the amount of disk space you've used and the amount of disk space you still have free.

🗀 K:

MAP NETWORK DRIVES
WITH NT EXPLORER ➤ *pp. 147-148*

Start NT Explorer. Choose the Tools | Map Network Drive command. In the Map Network Drive dialog box, specify which disk drive letter NT Explorer should use to represent the soon-to-be-mapped network drive and provide the computer name and the shared drive name.

Console

USE THE MS-DOS
COMMAND PROMPT ➤ *pp. 149-150*

Click the Start button. Then choose the Programs | Command Prompt command. NT starts MS-DOS and opens the console window. Issue commands the same way you do in MS-DOS.

🔑 6/6/96
🔒 6/6/96
🔒 6/6/96

START THE EVENT VIEWER ➤ *pp. 154-157*

Click Start. Then choose the Programs | Administrative Tools | Event Viewer command. Event Viewer lists events from one of three logs: the system log, the security log, and the application log. Double-click an event log entry to see a detailed description of the event.

Despite its reputation to the contrary, NT really is easy to use. Or, at least, it is easy to use now that it has the Windows 95 interface, look, and feel. But that much said, you aren't going to be surprised to read that NT possesses a massive amount of horsepower—power that you can tap into once you're proficient using the interface and ready for a little adventure.

In this chapter, I'm going to describe how you tap this horsepower by using NT's power user tools. I'm not going to describe all of NT's power user tools in this chapter—that would require several hundred pages. I can, however, explain in detail how you use three of the most useful and important power user tools: Windows NT Explorer, the NT command prompt, and the Event Viewer. In addition, I'll briefly describe three other power user tools: the Back Up, Disk Administrator, and Windows NT Diagnostics program.

USING WINDOWS NT EXPLORER

In Chapter 4, I describe how you use the My Computer program to work with and view your disks and files. It turns out that My Computer is actually a scaled-down version of another, more powerful program: the Windows NT Explorer. (To make your reading a bit less wordy, I'm just going to call it the NT Explorer from here on out.)

NT Explorer Basics

To start NT Explorer, click the Start button. Then choose the Programs | Windows NT Explorer command. NT starts NT Explorer and displays its program window (see Figure 8.1). As Figure 8.1 shows, NT Explorer shows a picture of your computer, emphasizing its disks, folders, and files but also showing any network disks you've mapped (or connected to), any printers you've added, the network neighborhood, and your briefcase.

You'll find it easiest to learn NT Explorer if you already know how the My Computer and Network Neighborhood programs work. For this reason, I urge you to read Chapter 4 if you're not already familiar with these other two programs.

Exploring - My Computer

Name	Type	Total Size	Free Space
3½ Floppy (A:)	3½ Inch Floppy Disk		
Big-gig (C:)	Local Disk	1.19GB	221MB
(D:)	CD-ROM Disc	223MB	0 bytes
Nt-gig (E:)	Local Disk	1.51GB	1.50GB
C$ on 'gigantor' (F:)	Network Connection	1.09GB	186MB
C$ on 'Gopher' (G:)	Network Connection	0.98GB	599MB
d$ on 'Gopher' (H:)	Network Connection	0.98GB	515MB
C$ on 'gigantor' (I:)	Network Connection	1.09GB	186MB
denola on 'enola' (J:)	Network Connection	1.00GB	250MB
Control Panel	System Folder		
Printers	System Folder		
Dial-Up Networking	System Folder		

12 object(s)

Figure 8.1 The Windows NT Explorer program window uses a tree diagram to show your computer's resources

habits & strategies

The My Briefcase program lets you easily move sets of files between two computers. You would typically use My Briefcase to move files from and to a laptop computer running Windows 95. If you have questions about My Briefcase, refer to your Windows 95 user documentation.

Take a couple of minutes to look over the program window shown in Figure 8.1. The left side of the window shows the folders pane. It shows a tree diagram of your disks, any network disks, the Control Panel folder, the Printers folder, the Network Neighborhood icon, the Recycle Bin folder, and the My Briefcase folder.

The right side of the window shows the folder contents list. If you select a disk or folder in the folders pane (including the Recycle Bin folder), the folder contents list shows the folders and files stored on or in your selection. If you select the Control Panel folder, the folder contents list shows the Control Panel tools. If you select the Printers folder, the folder contents list shows the Add Printer Wizard shortcut and the printers you've already added. If you select the Network Neighborhood icon, the folder contents list shows the computers in your workgroup and the domains in your network. Finally, if you select the My Briefcase folder, the folder contents list displays a list of the files stored in My Briefcase.

I know it sounds sort of kooky, but go ahead and click on the different icons you see in the folders pane. Click on a disk. Click on the Control Panel folder. Click on the Printers folder. See how the folder contents list changes? Okay, good.

You've perhaps noticed that some of the branches in the folders pane show little boxes with plus symbols in them:

These plus symbols indicate that the disk has folders or that a folder has a subfolder. Or, in other words, the branch has branches. If you click the plus symbol, NT expands the branch:

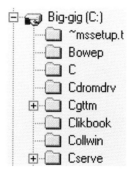

Notice that NT Explorer changes the branch's plus symbol to a minus symbol after you've expanded a branch. You can collapse the branch by clicking the minus symbol.

As long as you're not freaked or anything by all the information that NT Explorer shows on your screen (and I understand people who are freaked out) you'll really find NT Explorer the most expeditious way to work with disks, folders, files, and printers. With NT Explorer, you have everything in one place. Also with NT Explorer, you easily move between network resources (like mapped network drives and network printers) and local resources (like your computer's hard disk). Finally, with NT Explorer, you can also easily use shortcut icons that appear on the desktop (desktop shortcut icons appear in the folder contents list when the desktop is selected in the folders pane).

Working with Files and Folders

You can use NT Explorer to perform all of the file and folder management tasks that My Computer does—plus a bunch more. In the paragraphs that follow, I'll quickly describe a bunch of tasks that you can use NT Explorer for. But I'm not going to beat any horses to death. I figure that if you're reading a chapter with a title like this one, you're already at least passingly familiar with either My Computer or with NT Explorer's predecessors, the old File Manager and the old Program Manager.

Viewing a Disk's Contents

You can see the folders, or directories, you've used to organize a disk and view the files stored in those folders by double-clicking a disk's icon or a folder's icon in either the folders pane or the folder contents list. As in the case with the My Computer program (described in Chapter 4), two types of icons fill the folder contents list: folder icons and file icons. The icons that look like manila folders represent each of the folders, or directories, you or some program has created. The other icons represent program and document files.

If NT Explorer knows which program you used to create a file, it uses the program's icon as part of the file's icon. This sounds complicated, but take a look at the two file icons shown here:

Name	Size	Type
My great American novel	326KB	Microsoft Word Doc...
The Case of the Missing Heiress	5KB	Microsoft Word Doc...

Do you see how both icons show a big "W"? That's the Microsoft Word icon, which NT Explorer tacks onto the file icons to identify Word as the program used to create the file and that I can later use to work with the file.

Creating New Folders

You can use NT Explorer to easily add folders and subfolders. First select the disk or folder to which you want to add the new folder. Choose the File | New | Folder command. NT Explorer adds a new, unnamed folder and opens an editable text box over the new folder's default name, "New Folder":

Type the name you want to use for the new folder and press ENTER.

Opening Files

You can open a file you see in the NT Explorer window by double-clicking its icon. For example, if you double-click on a word processor document, NT starts the word processor program you used to create the document and then tells that program to open the file. If you open a program file, NT starts the program.

If NT Explorer doesn't know which program it's supposed to start so you can open a document file, it displays the Open With dialog box (shown in Figure 8.2). Select the program NT Explorer should use to open the file from the Choose the program you want to use list box. If you can't find the program listed, click the Other command button to display the standard Open dialog box (the same one you see when you choose the File | Open command from any NT program). Then use its Look in drop-down list box and its File name box to identify the program file.

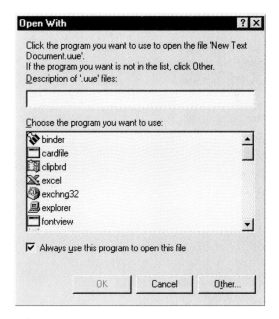

Figure 8.2 The Open With dialog box

If you want to free up additional disk space and you know you'll never want to undelete the files stored in the Recycle Bin, display the Recycle Bin folder and then choose its File | Empty Recycle Bin command.

Deleting and Undeleting Files

You can easily delete any document or program file you see in the folder contents list. (I'm not saying you *should* do this, by the way—only that you *can* easily do this.) To do this, right-click the file to display the shortcut menu and then choose the Delete command. Alternatively, press the DEL key. (You can also choose the File | Delete command, but that deletion technique isn't really worth reading about—and it's certainly not worth remembering.)

You usually can undelete any recently deleted file by opening the Recycle Bin folder, finding the file, right-clicking it (to display the shortcut menu), and then choosing the Restore command.

If you want to change the size of the Recycle Bin (and there's free space on your hard disk), right-click the Recycle Bin icon to display its shortcut menu. Choose the Properties command so that NT Explorer displays the Recycle Bin Properties dialog box (see Figure 8.3). To change the disk space allotted to the Recycle Bin, drag the slider button.

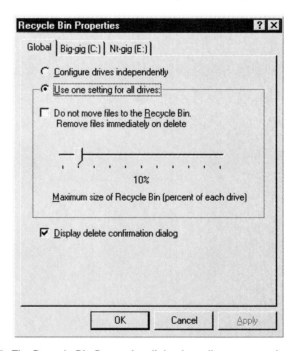

Figure 8.3 The Recycle Bin Properties dialog box allows you to change the size of the recycle bin

If you drag a file to a floppy disk's folder (without holding down the CTRL key), NT Explorer doesn't move the file. It copies the file.

SHORTCUT

A quick way to copy a file to a floppy disk is to right-click the file and then choose the Send To | Floppy command from the shortcut menu.

To change the way NT Explorer shows folders and files, you use the View | Large Icons, View | Small Icons, and View | List commands. For more information, refer to Chapter 10.

If you like to live life on the edge and don't need second chances, mark the check box that says Do not move files to the Recycle Bin. And then pray you don't make silly mistakes.

There's really no reason I can think of for you to fool around with any of the other boxes or buttons shown. But if you do have a question, click the question button shown in the upper-left corner of the dialog box and then click the thing you're curious about.

Renaming Files and Folders

To rename a file or folder shown in the folder contents list, select the file or folder and then click the file name. Then, when NT Explorer opens a text box over the file name, type the new name you want to use for the file. You can use letters, numbers, spaces, and most special characters in your name. There are a handful of characters you can't use, but I'm not going to list them here. If you use an illegal character, NT Explorer will tell you that what you've done isn't kosher.

Copying and Moving Files

Copying and moving files with NT Explorer saves time compared to copying and moving files with My Computer. To move a file with NT Explorer, drag it from one folder to another folder. (You may need to expand more than one branch of the tree diagram shown in the folders pane before doing this.) To copy a file with NT Explorer, hold down the CTRL key and then drag it from one folder to another folder.

If you want to copy or move a bunch of files, you have several ways to select multiple files. You can hold down the CTRL key and then individually click each file. You can hold down the SHIFT key and click the first and then the last file in a list of files you want. Finally, you can draw a rectangle around the files you want to select by dragging the mouse from one corner of the rectangle to the other, as shown here:

Formatting Floppy Disks

To format a floppy disk with NT Explorer, insert the floppy disk into the floppy disk drive. Right-click on the floppy disk icon to display its shortcut menu. Then choose the Format command. When NT displays the Format disk dialog box, shown in Figure 8.4, use the Capacity drop-down list box to specify the floppy disk type and density. Then click the Start button.

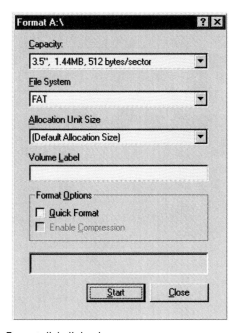

Figure 8.4 The Format disk dialog box

Monitoring Disk Space

NT Explorer lets you easily monitor the available disk space on both floppy disks and hard disks. Just right-click the disk you're concerned (or at least curious) about. Choose the Properties command from the shortcut menu. NT displays the disk's Properties dialog box, which uses a pie chart to show you the amount of disk space you've used and the amount of disk space you still have free.

If you find your disk is almost

full, you've got three options.

You can move files to another

disk (described earlier in the

chapter). You can delete files

you don't need (also described

earlier). Or you can have

someone add another hard disk

to your computer.

Mapping Network Drives

If a network drive doesn't show up in the folders pane—and you want it to—you'll need to map the drive. To do this, choose the Tools | Map Network Drive command. When NT Explorer displays the Map Network Drive dialog box, shown in Figure 8.5, use it to specify which disk drive letter NT Explorer should use to represent the soon-to-be-mapped network drive and provide the computer name and the shared drive name.

Figure 8.5 The Map Network Drive dialog box

Typically, you will accept the drive letter that NT Explorer suggests and shows in the Drive drop-down list box. NT Explorer just assigns the next available drive letter to the mapped network drive, and this is probably what you want. For example, in Figure 8.5, NT Explorer suggests the letter K be used to represent the next network drive because I've already used the letters A and B for floppy drives, the letters C, D, and E for hard and CD-ROM drives, and the letters F, G, H, I, and J for previously mapped network drives.

Use the Path box to enter the computer name and the shared folder name using the form **\\computername\foldername**. For example, if you want to map to the folder shared as C$ on the computer named gopher, you enter **\\gopher\C$** in the path box (see Figure 8.5 for an example of how this works).

The Map Network Drive dialog box also provides two other options: the Connect As box and the Reconnect at Logon check box. You typically shouldn't have to worry about the Connect As box. It lets

you connect to a shared folder as another user. If you want, you can mark the Reconnect at Logon check box. This tells NT to reconnect to the network drive whenever you log on (your logon will take slightly longer, but if you're going to be grabbing stuff from a bunch of different network drives, you may as well reconnect to them all at once when you log on and get this work out of the way).

Disconnecting Network Drives

If you're not going to be using files from a particular network drive, there's no reason so stay connected. Staying connected to a bunch of unneeded network drives clutters the NT Explorer window. And it does increase the time NT takes to start up (even if ever so slightly). To disconnect a network drive, choose the Tools | Disconnect Network Drive command. When NT Explorer displays the Disconnect Network Drive dialog box (see Figure 8.6), use the Network Drive list box to select the network drive you no longer need to use. Then click OK.

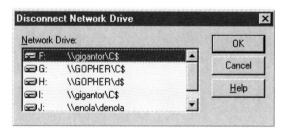

Figure 8.6 The Disconnect Network Drive dialog box lets you disconnect previously mapped network drives

Using the Network Neighborhood

NT Explorer lets you view a graphical picture of your neighborhood, called the Network Neighborhood. I talked about Network Neighborhood in Chapter 4. (I rather loosely described Network Neighborhood as a "program," which isn't quite true. It's really just a set of windows that let you view the computers and other resources connected to a network.) So I'm not going to talk about how Network Neighborhood works when you get to it from NT Explorer. It works the same way no matter how you get there.

Using the Printers Folder

If you open the Printers folder using NT Explorer, NT Explorer displays the same Printers window that NT does when you click the Start button and then choose the Settings | Printers command. I describe in detail how you work with the Printers window and the individual printer's folders in Chapter 5. Refer to that chapter if you have questions.

Using the Control Panel Folder

The Control Panel folder lists a bunch of tools—basically small programs—you can use to customize the way NT works and looks. Chapter 10, "Customizing NT Workstations," describes how several of the more useful (in my opinion) Control Panel tools work. Refer there if you have questions.

USING THE MS-DOS COMMAND PROMPT

NT will run the MS-DOS operating system. This sounds funny—and it is, if you think about it for more than about a minute. But it's true. NT *will* run the old MS-DOS operating system. Now, while most users should get just as fast and as far away from MS-DOS as they possibly can, some users will want MS-DOS. And, perhaps, not just Luddites. If you've got MS-DOS-based programs, for example, you can start MS-DOS and then use it to start these other programs. (You can also start most MS-DOS programs directly from NT, but let's not be picky.) Or, if you like working at the MS-DOS command prompt—say you think this whole graphical user interface thing is just a passing fad—you can start MS-DOS to get its command prompt.

Starting and Using the Command Prompt

To start MS-DOS, click the Start button. Then choose the Programs | Command Prompt command. When you do, NT starts MS-DOS and opens the console window, as shown in Figure 8.7. Ah yes, you remember now: the highly illegible white-text-on-a-black-background scheme.

To be totally precise, NT actually provides an MS-DOS emulator—not MS-DOS itself. What's more, the window you open when you click on the MS-DOS Command Prompt icon doubles as both the NT command line console and a place to run DOS, WIN16, and WIN32 programs.

Figure 8.7 Use the console window to issue MS-DOS style commands

habits & strategies

*To see a list of the MS-DOS commands you can issue using the console window, type **help**. To see information about using a specific command, type **help** followed by the name of the command. For example, to get information about the start command, type **help start**.*

NT provides many commands beyond those available in MS-DOS.

Once the console window appears, you issue commands the same way you do in MS-DOS. You type the command (including any little extra bits of information the command needs). For example, if you want to see a list of the folders and files in the active directory, type **dir**. Then press ENTER. That's it.

Actually, that's not really it, because there are about 70 MS-DOS commands you can type. You can also type any program name to start that program. And you can type any batch file name to execute the commands or programs listed in the *batch file* (a text file that lists a bunch of commands or programs).

If you're really interested in using the command prompt to do a bunch of different stuff, what you want to do is learn as much about the MS-DOS style of working as you can. Because that's the style and syntax you're really using. Find a good (or at least a decent) book on MS-DOS. If your computer came with a guide to MS-DOS, you may be able to use that. Or, if you're really serious about all of this, you might want to get a big reference book on MS-DOS. I wouldn't get one of those DOS-lite books—like *DOS for Dummies*—because when you want more information about a particular command, you're going to want lots of detailed coverage.

To stop the MS-DOS operating system and close the console window, type **exit** at the command prompt. (You will need to first stop any MS-DOS programs you've started.)

Copying and Pasting Data to and from a Console Window

You can copy and paste data between a program you've started with the console window and another Windows-based program you've started, say, from the Programs menu.

To copy some bit of data shown in the console window and then paste it into a regular NT program window, first click the console window's control menu icon (the little icon in the upper-left corner of the window) so that NT activates the console window's control menu:

Next, choose the Edit | Mark command and select the data you want to copy, such as by dragging the mouse. Activate the console window's control menu again and choose the Edit | Copy command. At this point, you've copied the data to the NT Clipboard. To move the data from the Clipboard to some other program, make that program window the active one, move the selection cursor to wherever you want to place the data, and choose that program's Edit | Paste command.

To copy data shown in a regular NT program window to the console window, select the data you want to copy, such as by dragging the mouse. Choose the program's Edit | Copy command. At this point, you've copied the data to the NT Clipboard. To move the data to the console window, make the console window the active program window, move the cursor to where you want the data placed (if necessary). And then activate the console window's control menu and choose the Edit | Paste command.

Customizing the Console Window

I'm going to talk in detail about customizing NT in Chapter 10, but rather than wait until then, let me quickly tell you about some of the customizations you can make to the console window from the MS-DOS command prompt. By placing this information here rather than in Chapter 10, I won't confuse those readers who aren't interested in using the MS-DOS command prompt.

To customize the console window, click the Start button. Then choose the Settings | Control Panel command so that NT displays the Control Panel window. If the NT Explorer window shows, you can also click the Control Panel folder in the folders pane to display the Control Panel window. Next, double-click the MS-DOS Console tool:

Console

When you do, NT displays the Console Windows Properties dialog box (see Figure 8.8). You can use it to change the size of the console window, the font NT uses inside the window, the size of the window, and its colors.

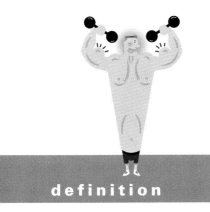

definition

Buffer: *A temporary storage place—a scratch pad, in effect—used for holding computer data.*

The Options tab, for example, lets you make a bunch of eclectic specifications concerning the console window. The Cursor Size buttons let you specify the cursor size as small (the usual case), medium, or large. The Display Options buttons let you specify whether the console should appear in a window or use the full screen (the Display Options buttons are available only on Intel-based computers and not on RISC-based computers). The Command History boxes let you specify how many previously issued commands NT should save in a buffer, and it lets you tell NT that it can discard duplicate commands. The Insert Mode check box tells NT whether pasted data should be inserted at the insertion point location or should replace, or overtype, text starting at the insertion point location. Finally, the QuickEdit Mode check box tells NT that you don't have time to fool around with the console window's control menu Edit | Mark command and want to be able to just drag the mouse to make selections whenever and wherever you want.

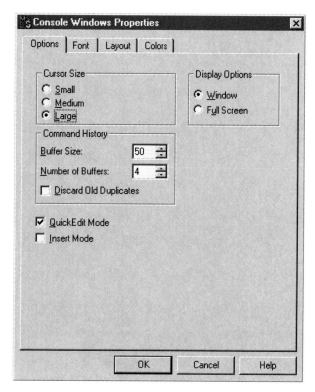

Figure 8.8 The Console Windows Properties dialog box lets you specify how the console window should work and look

The Font tab in the Console Windows Properties dialog box lets you choose which font you want NT to use within the console window. You shouldn't have much trouble figuring out how to select the options in this tab. Use the Font list box to pick the font you want. Use the Size list box to pick the point size (for your information, a point is 1/72 of an inch). The Font tab provides a preview box to see what your font selection looks like.

The Layout tab, which also appears on the Console Windows Properties dialog box, lets you tell NT how big the console window should be and where it should appear. You can't hurt anything by experimenting with the boxes and buttons that this tab provides. So go ahead, get crazy. And use the preview box to see what your layout specification looks like.

The Console Windows Properties dialog box provides one other tab, called Colors. You use the Colors tab, shown in Figure 8.9, to specify the screen text and background colors and the pop-up window text and background colors. If you're sick to death of white text on a black background, this is the place to make your stand.

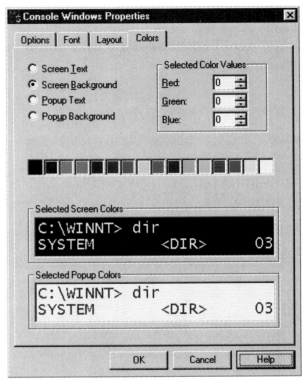

Figure 8.9 The Colors tab lets you get wild and crazy on your console window (but only if you want to)

CAUTION

All events get recorded in the Event Viewer logs. Some events are so urgent or important that NT also displays message boxes.

USING EVENT VIEWER

Event Viewer maintains a log—a written record—of significant system events and problems: device drivers that NT attempts to start but can't (like the one needed for your CD-ROM drive), services that NT attempts to start but can't (like the ones needed so you can use your corporate e-mail service), and security events (like someone trying to use a file they're not supposed to). For these reasons, when you experience operating system or hardware difficulties or when you're monitoring system security, you'll use Event Viewer. Note, though, that you don't use Event Viewer to solve these sorts of problems. You use Event Viewer to research these problems so you can fix them with other tools.

Starting and Using the Event Viewer

To start Event Viewer, click Start. Then choose the Programs | Administrative Tools | Event Viewer command. NT starts Event Viewer and displays its program window (see Figure 8.10). The Event Viewer program lists events from one of three logs:

- the system log (which is the default log and is shown in Figure 8.10)
- the security log (which reports security events)
- and the application log (which reports application events)

NT records three types of events in its system log:

- information events ("i" in a blue dot icon)
- warning events (exclamation point in a yellow dot icon)
- error events (red stop sign icon).

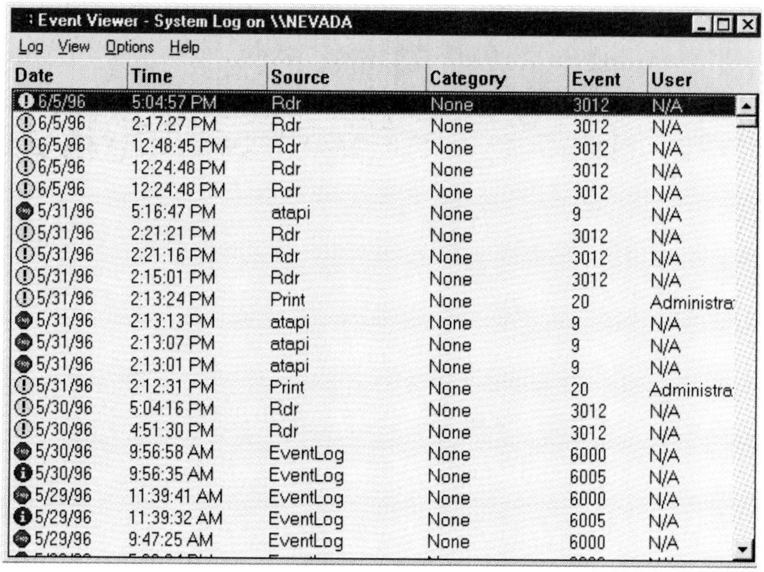

Figure 8.10 The Event Viewer log showing system events

Just for fun, take another peek at Figure 8.10 to make sure you can spot one of each type of event.

Okay, here's the next thing you should know. People like you and me probably won't ever fool around with the system log. At least not on our own. At a technical support engineer's direction, however, we might hunt through this log looking for an error event (like the sixth event listed in Figure 8.10). The red stop sign icon indicates that this is a serious event—probably a device failure of some sort. The technical support engineer would probably next ask you to double-click the event to display a more lengthy description of the error. Figure 8.11 shows the full event description for a serious event occurring on 5/31/96 from the atapi source. Whatever that is.

You're probably not going to know what the event description information shown in Figure 8.11 even means. But with this information, someone who does know what atapi source is (it's the device driver your computer needs to connect to some types of disk drives) can help you get your system working again.

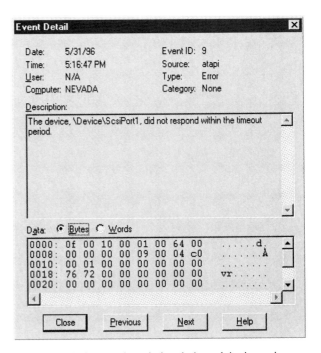

Figure 8.11   The detailed event description: it doesn't look good

I know this sounds like funny advice, but don't worry about the system log stuff you see in Figures 8.10 and 8.11. You just need to know how to get to the Event Viewer, double-click the event descriptions, and read the stuff shown in the Event Detail dialog box. You're not going to know what to do with this information unless you happen to have encountered the same problem before. If it makes you feel any better, the Microsoft technical support engineers who help you solve these sorts of problems are basically all computer science graduates and have gone through about six months of training.

Using the Application Log

The application log looks like the system log. It also works the same way. It differs in that it reports on problems with application programs you've started, such as your word processor, and not on problems with the operating system. You might be called on to review this log as part of helping some poor application technical support person address a program bug.

Using the Security Log

You know all that stuff I just said about the system log and application log being too complicated for mere mortals to deal with? While I think that's true for those two event logs, the story differs for the security log. The security log reports on all the security events the administrator says should be audited—including successful or failed file operations, if file owners want to audit this sort of stuff.

To view the security log, start Event Viewer and choose the Log | Security command. Event Viewer displays the security log shown in Figure 8.12. You've probably already noticed that NT uses different icons to flag security events. The key icon identifies successful security events, such as someone successfully logging onto the system. The padlock icon identifies failed security events, such as someone trying unsuccessfully to log onto the system or trying to open a file without having permission to read the file.

Figure 8.13 shows the event description for the first failed security event shown in Figure 8.12. What it reports is that someone (me) tried to log on the computer named Nevada using the user name "Administrator" but couldn't because the correct password wasn't provided (a

Many readers will have an empty security log, since most auditing features are disabled by default.

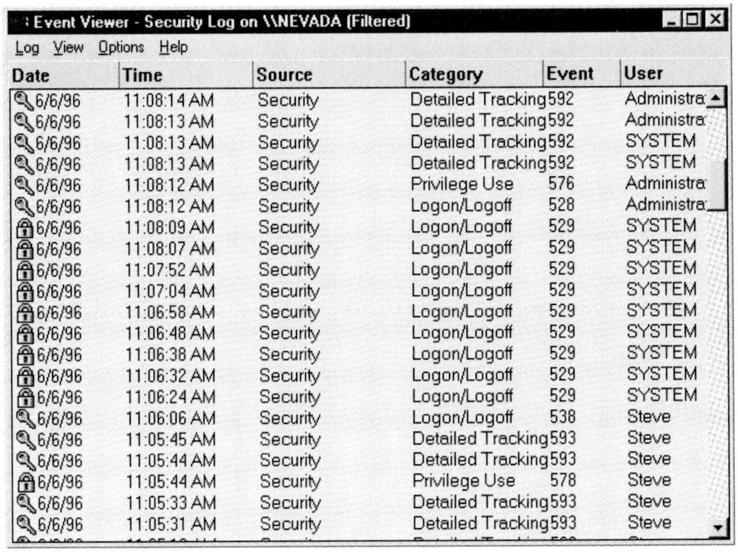

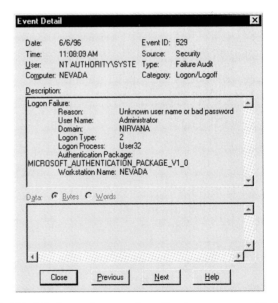

Figure 8.12 The security log provides an audit trail of security events, such

Figure 8.13 This failed security event describes how someone tried to log on with either a bad user name or a bad password

coworker with an interesting sense of humor changed the Administrator password without telling me).

A Few More Comments About Event Viewer

You actually know everything you need to know about the Event Viewer program and how to use it. You know what it does, for example. You know how to flip between the three event logs. And you know how to get the detailed event descriptions that you or others may need to solve some problem. If I were you, I'd probably just skip to the next section on other power user tools.

But you're not me. You want to know just a bit more about how the Event Viewer program works. So let me do that here. In machine-gun fashion, I will describe three tasks that frequent Event Viewer users will want to perform.

Saving and Opening Event Logs

NT erases old event log information. In fact, the default setting is for NT to erase event log information older than seven days. If you want to keep event log information, however, you can do so. Just choose the Log | Save As command. When Event Viewer displays the Save As dialog box, use the Save in drop-down list box to specify where you want the event log file saved, and use the File name box to give the event log file a name.

To later open an event log file, choose the Log | Open command. When Event Viewer displays the Open dialog box, use the Look in drop-down list box to specify where you saved the event log file, and use the File name box to identify the event log file. Click OK. Event Viewer will then ask whether you want to open the system log, the security log, or the application log.

Log Housekeeping

If you want to specify how Event Viewer gets rid of old events, choose the Log | Log Settings command. Event Viewer displays the Event Log Settings dialog box:

habits & strategies

Before you clear a log, you'll usually want to save the log to disk using the Log | Save As command.

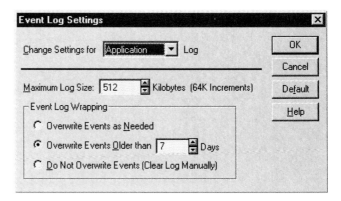

In the dialog box, specify how Event Viewer should log events. First, specify which event log you want to affect using the Change Settings for drop-down list box. Use the Maximum Log Size box to set a limit on the log's length. And use the Event Log Wrapping option buttons to specify what Event Viewer should do when the log gets full.

You can also manually clear the log by choosing the Log | Clear All Events command.

Filtering, Sorting, and Finding Events

If your logs get really lengthy and clogged with events, you can use the View | Filter Events command to display the Filter dialog box:

habits & strategies

To later remove a filter, choose

the View | All Events command.

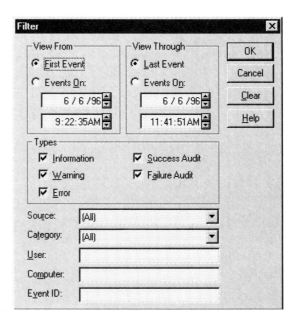

CAUTION

I'm not providing an exhaustive list of all of NT's almost hidden and invariably esoteric programs and utilities here. I'm describing only those you'll encounter on a menu or hear about from a technical support engineer or hardware repair person.

The Filter dialog box lets you filter events based on the type of event, the event date, and the source and category of the event.

You can use the View | Newest First and the View | Oldest First commands to sort the events by date and time.

Finally, one last point. If you choose the View | Find command, Event Viewer displays the Find dialog box, which you may be able to use to locate a specific event you're looking for; you'll probably need to know more about system, security, and application events than I've described here, however, to use this command and dialog box with any precision.

MORE POWER USER TOOLS

NT supplies a handful of other programs that you won't read about here. I'm skipping them because I am very confident that you, as a busy person, don't want to read about them. If you would have wanted an 800-page book on NT, you would have purchased the 800-page book, right?

Okay, with that inauspicious introduction, let me say that NT supplies three other programs that some very sophisticated users and other very unfortunate users may end up using: Back Up, Disk Administrator, and Windows NT Diagnostics.

Using the Back Up Program

The Back Up program, which appears on the Administrative Tools submenu of the Programs menu, backs up the contents of one or more disks or folders to a tape drive. While you should religiously back up your data, you never want to use this program. I hate backing up to tape. It's slow. It's unreliable if you leave the tapes sitting around for more than a few weeks (which of course is what happens in a small network like ours). And, personally, I find the tape backup software unnecessarily complex. So what you want to do is either get the network administrator to back up your data or back up to a high-density removable disk (like a Syquest Cartridge, an Iomega Zip drive, a floptical disk, or something else that sounds like one of these).

By the way, I think you should back up a few of your more important files onto a floppy disk. Maybe I'm a weenie, but I get nervous when I've only got one or two copies of an important file (like a chapter of this book) or an important set of files (like the figure images for this chapter). You can usually fit these ever-so-important files on a floppy

*If you want your network
administrator to back up your
data, you may need to keep your
data in a shared, network
directory for this to happen.
Ask the network administrator
for details.*

disk or two. If need be, you can also use a third-party compression utility to scrunch the file or files so they take less space. You can order a 32-bit version of Nico Mak Computing's WinZip utility by calling (713) 524-6394 during normal business hours.

Using Disk Administrator

The Disk Administrator program also appears on the Administrative Tools submenu of the Programs menu. While its visibility may make it seem like a program you should use, the only reason that people like you and I would use the Disk Administrator would be to partition a new hard disk. But I say pay the person who installs the hard disk an extra $5 and let him or her do it.

Using Windows NT Diagnostics

You can use the Windows NT Diagnostics program, which also appears on the Administrative Tools submenu of the Programs menu, to get all sorts of detailed information about your computer: which IRQs are used for which devices, what DMA channels devices are using, which services are running, and so forth. In real life, someone would only use this program in two situations: when installing a new piece of hardware and when troubleshooting some NT operating system problem or hardware glitch. I only do this kind of stuff when I absolutely have to. Most people won't want to be bothered.

ON FROM HERE

As it's installed, NT works pretty well. But you can do things to make its programs run more smoothly and to make it use your computer's resources more efficiently. Chapter 10 describes how to perform this sort of performance tuning. Not now, but when you have time, consider reading it.

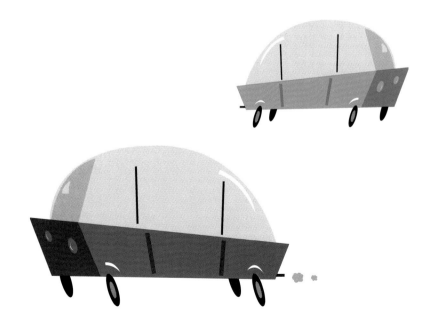

Using the Internet with Windows NT

INCLUDES

- Connecting to the Internet with NT

- Starting the Internet Explorer

- Browsing the World Wide Web

FAST FORWARD

CONNECT TO THE INTERNET WITH NT ➤ *pp. 167-168*

To connect to the World Wide Web, install NT's Internet Jumpstart Kit. It provides a recent copy of Microsoft's Internet Explorer, which is a Web browser. You'll also need to configure either a proxy server or an NT remote access service (RAS) connection.

START INTERNET EXPLORER ➤ *p. 168*

If you've got a proxy server, all you probably have to do is start the Internet Explorer program, usually by double-clicking its shortcut icon. If you're using a RAS connection, you need to make the connection first; once you've made the connection, start Internet Explorer.

**BROWSE THE WORLD WIDE WEB
WITH INTERNET EXPLORER ➤** *pp. 169-174*

You move among Web pages by clicking on hyperlinks with your mouse. By clicking on a hyperlink—which can be a chunk of text or a picture—you tell your Web browser to move you to another Web page.

definition

Web Browser: lets you view World Wide Web documents.

Windows NT 4.0 comes with Microsoft's Internet Jumpstart Kit. With the Internet Jumpstart Kit, you get Internet Explorer, which lets you browse the World Wide Web, read and post newsgroup messages, connect to FTP servers and gopher servers, and even make Telnet connections. I can't describe everything about the Internet or Internet Explorer in a single, short chapter like this. But I can explain how you start. If you get into this thing and decide you want more information, might I be so bold as to mention something? I've written another book, entitled *The World Wide Web for Busy People* (Osborne/McGraw-Hill, 1996), and it talks in detail about how you use Web browsers such as Internet Explorer to browse the World Wide Web and use other Internet services.

CONNECTING TO THE INTERNET WITH NT

habits & strategies

The Internet Jumpstart Kit comes with NT—another one of NT's freebie accessories. If you (or the administrator) didn't install the kit when installing NT, then you'll need to do so before continuing.

To connect to the World Wide Web, you'll need to install NT's Internet Jumpstart Kit. It provides a recent copy of Microsoft's Web browser, called Internet Explorer.

Fortunately, installing the Internet Jumpstart Kit isn't difficult if NT is already installed. Insert the Windows NT Workstation 4.0 distribution CD into your computer's CD drive. The NT Installation program should start and display the Windows NT CD-ROM window. Click the Add/Remove Software button so that the installation program displays the Add/Remove Programs Properties dialog box. Double-click the Accessories item in the list box that appears on the Windows NT Setup tab on the Add/Remove Programs Properties dialog box (click this tab if it doesn't already show). The installation program displays the Accessories dialog box. Scroll down its Components list box, marking the

Internet Jumpstart Kit entry when you come to it. Click OK to close the Accessories dialog box. Click OK to close the Add/Remove Programs Properties dialog box. At this point, you've installed the Internet Explorer.

Before you can use the Internet Explorer, however, you'll need to either configure a proxy server or set up a remote access service (RAS) connection (also called a Dial-Up Networking connection). You use a proxy server if the network on which you work connects to the Internet. If you're going to go this route, ask the network administrator for information on how you do this. You use a RAS (pronounced "razz") connection if you're connecting to the Internet using a modem and an Internet service provider (such as Microsoft Network). Again, you'll probably need someone else to help you do this. For someone to set up a RAS connection, he or she needs to know both how RAS works and how the Internet service provider wants people to connect to the service.

Once you've got a proxy server or RAS connection set up, starting the Internet Explorer (so you can access the Internet) is easy. If you've got a proxy server, all you usually have to do is start the Internet Explorer program—probably by double-clicking its shortcut icon, which should appear on the Windows NT desktop:

habits & strategies

If you want or need to configure your RAS connection yourself, take the time to read through the Windows NT documentation. And get any information you can—preferably detailed instructions—from the Internet service provider.

If you're using a RAS connection, you need to make the connection first. Ask whomever set up the RAS connection how you should do this. And then, once you've made the connection, start Internet Explorer.

BROWSING THE WORLD WIDE WEB WITH INTERNET EXPLORER

The first Web page you see after you connect to the Internet is called your *home page,* or start page. Typically, your home page resides (is stored) on the Web server provided by your Internet service provider. But you can use any Web page for a home page. If you're using Microsoft's corporate web sites as your home page, for example, it might look something like the one shown in Figure 9.1.

Using Hyperlinks to Move Between Web Pages

With any Web browser, you move among Web pages by clicking on hyperlinks with your mouse. By clicking on a hyperlink—which can

Figure 9.1 The first page your Web browser displays is called a home page, or start page

CAUTION

Web page designs change incessantly. So don't expect the Web pages shown in this chapter to look identical to what you see on your screen. By the time you view them, the Web pages I show here will almost surely have changed.

be a chunk of text or a picture—you tell your Web browser to move you to another Web page. For example, let's say you click on the Products hyperlink from Figure 9.1 shown here:

Products

Your Web browser then displays the Web page shown in Figure 9.2.

Hyperlinks can be a little tricky, in that they don't always stand out on a Web page. In Figure 9.1, for example, things are pretty clear. You can probably guess that the row of buttons at the top are clickable and are therefore hyperlinks. But take a close look at Figure 9.2. Or, better yet, take a close look at your screen if you're following along in front of your computer. You'll notice that some of the text (like the Products hyperlink) appears in a different color if you're working on a color monitor. These colored chunks of text also represent hyperlinks.

Internet Explorer changes the mouse pointer to a hand with an extended pointer finger whenever you point to a hyperlink.

Figure 9.2 Here's what you see after you click the Products hyperlink

If you're connecting to the Internet with a RAS connection and you're following along at your computer, you've probably learned a dirty little secret of the Internet and, in particular, the World Wide Web: it's slow. Even if you've got a super-fast modem, you'll spend most of your time waiting for some distant Web server to transmit the Web page you've requested by clicking its hyperlink. You shouldn't get discouraged by this new bit of information, however— what you need to do is minimize the time you spend waiting for useless information.

Paging to Previous or Next Web Page

You can page back and forth to the Web pages you've already viewed by clicking the Back and Forward buttons:

One thing you'll notice if you do this (go ahead and try it right now) is that redisplaying a page you've already viewed takes only a split second.

The reason you can quickly redisplay Web pages you've recently viewed, by the way, is that your Web browser actually stores, or *caches,* a copy of the Web page on your computer's hard disk. So when you redisplay a Web page, your Web browser only has to go to the work of grabbing the file from your hard disk—a very fast operation—rather than taking the file from some distant Web server.

If you want your Web browser to grab a new copy of a Web page rather than one from its cache, you click the Refresh button:

You might want to do this, for example, if a Web page displays information that is continually (or almost continually) updated: Web

habits & strategies

You don't need to wait until your browser finishes retrieving a Web page before you click a new hyperlink or page back and forth. You can stop retrieving one page and move to another page at any time.

pages linked to cameras that continually take new pictures, weather maps that get updated based on new satellite data, and so forth.

If a Web page is taking too long to load, you can always tell Internet Explorer to give up. To do this, click the Stop button:

Creating and Using Favorite Places

The Internet uses painfully cryptic addresses called URLs (uniform resource locators) to identify the precise locations of Web sites and their Web pages. For example, the URL for Microsoft Corporation's Web site is the following:

```
http://www.microsoft.com/
```

And General Motors' is the following:

```
http://www.gm.com
```

If you know a Web site's URL, you can type it directly into the Address box. Just be careful about spelling and typographical mistakes—like using back-slashes in place of slashes or commas in place of periods.

If you work with the World Wide Web very much, you'll want to learn how to work with these URLs. But even after you do, you'll still find it really useful to have your browser memorize often-visited Web page addresses. Internet Explorer calls these memorized addresses Favorite Places. To tell Internet Explorer to memorize the current Web server or Web page address, choose the Favorites | Add Favorite command. To later view a Web page you've marked as a favorite, activate the Favorites menu and then choose the memorized Web page you want to view from the menu.

Saving Content

You can usually save the information shown in the browser window. This means that if some Web page shows a picture, you can save the picture. And if some Web page has a bunch of textual information—maybe it's an article on moving to the south of France—you can save that, too.

Saving the Textual Portion of a Web Page

To save the textual portion of a Web page, choose the File | Save As command. When Internet Explorer displays the Save As dialog box (see Figure 9.3), use the list boxes to specify where Internet Explorer should save a file that contains the textual portion of the Web page. Use the Format box to specify that you just want "plain text" saved. Then use the Save As box to name the text file you're creating. When you finish all this, click Save.

Saving Graphic Images

To save a graphic image shown in a Web page, choose the File | Save As command. When Internet Explorer displays the Save As dialog box (see Figure 9.3), use the list boxes to specify where Internet Explorer should save the file. Use the Format box to specify that you just want the file saved in its "source" format. Then use the Save As box to name the file. When you finish all this, click Save.

Downloading Files

Some hyperlinks don't point to other Web pages. They point to files. When you click one of these hyperlinks, what you're really telling Internet Explorer to do is *download,* or retrieve, the file from the Web

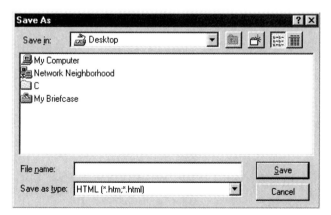

Figure 9.3 Use the Save As dialog box to name the file and specify where on your hard disk it should be stored

FTP is another Internet service. It moves files between computers connected to the Internet.

server or even another type of server, such as an FTP server. When you click one of these hyperlinks, you'll also have to use a Save As dialog box to indicate where Internet Explorer should save the file.

Forms Work Like Dialog Boxes

You need to know about just one other topic to easily work with the Web: how to use forms. Fortunately, if you've been working with NT for more than about a day or two, you already know how to do this. Forms are just Web pages that work and look like dialog boxes. They include check boxes and option buttons you mark, text boxes you fill in, and command buttons you click. You use forms to order products, play interactive games, register for online services, and enter data for Web calculators and search services.

CLOSING CAVEATS AND COMMENTS

Let me give you a couple of tips about learning and enjoying to use the Internet and the World Wide Web. First, learn the logic (madness?) of URLs (they start with prefixes like http://, ftp://, and so on). They aren't that difficult to learn. And once you understand how they work—information that can be provided in any good book on the Internet—you'll find a lot of your questions getting answered almost automatically.

Second, learn to use one of the Internet search services like the one at http://www.yahoo.com/ or the one at http://altavista.digital.com/. Search services let you find stuff on the Internet; without them, it's possible to waste hours—no, make that days—of time.

ON FROM HERE

This chapter and the previous two chapters (Chapters 7 and 8) have described some of the special programs that come with NT. The next (and final) two chapters, however, get back into the nitty-gritty details of the NT operating system. In Chapter 10, I describe how you can customize the way NT works and looks. In Chapter 11, I describe how you can performance-tune NT so it runs more smoothly and makes better and more efficient use of your computer's resources.

Customizing NT Workstations

INCLUDES

- Creating shortcuts and redecorating your desktop

- Customizing your menus

- Customizing NT Explorer and My Computer

- Adding and removing programs

- Changing regional settings

- Adjusting the system date and time

- Changing the keyboard and mouse settings

- Changing NT sounds

FAST FORWARD

CREATE SHORTCUTS ON
THE DESKTOP ➤ *pp. 180-182*

Open NT Explorer and size the window so that part of the desktop is showing. Open the folder with the item for which you want to create a shortcut. Then drag the icon, holding down the *right* mouse button, and drop it anywhere on the desktop where there's a blank space. When you let go of the button, NT displays a shortcut menu. Choose the Create Shortcut(s) Here command.

DELETE AND RENAME SHORTCUT ICONS ➤ *p. 182*

To delete a shortcut icon, select it and press the DEL key. To rename a shortcut icon, click the shortcut icon to select it. Then click on the name and type the new, replacement name.

CUSTOMIZE THE TASK BAR ➤ *pp. 187-188*

To change the task bar location, drag it to where you want it moved. To make changes to the task bar's appearance, click the Start button and choose the Settings | Taskbar command. When NT displays the Taskbar Properties dialog box, use it to make your changes.

Start Menu Programs

ADD SHORTCUTS TO MENUS ➤ *pp. 189-190*

To place a shortcut on the Start menu, start NT Explorer and open the folder that contains the program or document you want to add. Then, drag the program or document's icon to the Start button. To place a shortcut in a submenu, click the Start button and then choose the Settings | Taskbar command. When NT displays the Taskbar Properties dialog box, click on the Start Menu Programs tab and then the Add button. Use the Create Shortcut dialog box that NT displays to add the program or document to the menu you specify.

○ Show all files
● Hide files of these types:

Add/Remove
Programs

CUSTOMIZE NT EXPLORER
AND MY COMPUTER ➤ *pp. 190-194*

Use the View toolbar buttons and View menu commands to customize the way the NT Explorer program looks and the way it organizes information contained within its window. These same customizations can be applied to the My Computer program as well.

USE THE CONTROL PANEL'S TOOLS ➤ *pp. 194-202*

Use the Control Panel's tools to install new programs, remove programs you no longer need, change regional settings (such as the language), adjust the system date and time, customize the operation of the mouse and keyboard, and change the sounds that NT uses. To open the Control Panel, click the Start button and choose the Settings | Control Panel command.

You get a lot of control over your computer and the way it works from NT. It doesn't just allow you to control the surface things, either, like the desktop background. You also get control over more important things—like the ways you work with and start documents, the way you view your computer using the My Computer program or its cousin, NT Explorer, and even over mechanical things like the way that your mouse and keyboard operate.

Many people aren't going to want to exercise this control. And that's okay. But I will say this: knowing how to do all (or at least some) of this stuff should make your life easier and your computing more productive.

CREATING SHORTCUT ICONS FOR YOUR DESKTOP

A shortcut icon is just a clickable picture you can use for starting programs and opening documents. Initially, NT's desktop—which is usually, but not always, where these shortcut icons show up—provides three shortcut icons: one for the My Computer program, one for the Network Neighborhood icon, and one for the Recycle Bin folder. But you can add others—and you should consider doing so. You can even place a shortcut to a disk drive or folder on your desktop, like the following:

With this shortcut icon, you can copy a file to a disk simply by dragging the file's icon and dropping it on the shortcut to the disk drive.

To drag and drop a shortcut icon, place the mouse cursor over the icon, press a mouse button and, while still holding the button down, move the icon to a different location.

Creating Shortcuts on the Desktop

As an example, let's place a new shortcut to Microsoft Word on the desktop. To do this, open NT Explorer and size the window so that part of the desktop is showing, as in Figure 10.1.

In NT Explorer, open the Winword folder, which has the item (Windword.exe) item for which we want to create a shortcut. Then drag the item's icon, holding down the *right* mouse button, and drop it anywhere on the desktop. Don't worry about where. I'll explain how to tidy up the desktop in a second (in "Arranging Shortcut Icons").

When you let go of the button, NT displays a shortcut menu. Choose the Create Shortcut(s) Here command.

Shortcut icons look different than other icons. In the lower-left corner of the icon, NT adds a little white box with an arrow:

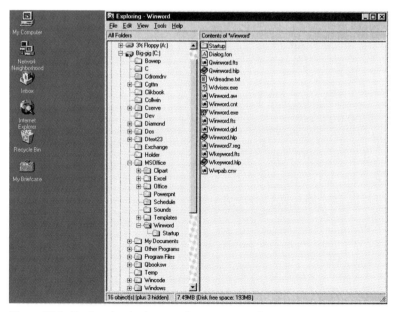

Figure 10.1 Getting the desktop ready to create a shortcut

CAUTION

The desktop is actually a special NT folder. Choosing to move a file instead of creating a shortcut to it (Move is one of the other commands on the shortcut menu) deletes it from the folder where it presently exists and moves it to the Desktop folder.

Compare the previous shortcut icon with the following regular one:

Deleting and Renaming Shortcut Icons

You can work with shortcut icons in the same ways that you work with regular folders and files. To delete a shortcut icon, for example, select it and press the DEL key. Or right-click it and choose the Delete command. Or just drag the icon to the Recycle Bin (this is probably the easiest way).

If you want to rename a shortcut icon, no problem. Click the shortcut icon to select it. Then click on the name, and NT will open an edit box for you to type the new name, as with the following:

Type the new name, then click anywhere else on the desktop to save the change.

Arranging Shortcut Icons

If you start adding shortcut icons to your desktop, things can get messy fast. Sort of like a teenager's room, I guess. Fortunately, NT provides some handy tools for arranging and rearranging the shortcut icons that appear on your desktop. Right-click in a blank area on the desktop so that the desktop shortcut menu appears.

If you just want to arrange all the icons into nice rows and columns, choose the Line Up Icons command, and NT will take care of it. Alternatively, choose the Arrange Icons command. Then, when NT displays the Arrange Icons submenu, choose the submenu command that describes the way you want shortcut icons arranged:

- By Name, of course, sorts the icons by their names.

- By Type divides the icons into groups according to whether they are a document, folder, or application, then sorts each group alphabetically by name.
- By Size sorts according to size. (In the case of shortcuts, it uses the size of the shortcut rather than the size of the original document.)
- By Date sorts according to the last date the document was saved.
- Auto Arrange works like an on-off switch. If you've turned the switch on, NT automatically re-sorts the icons whenever you change the desktop.

REDECORATING YOUR DESKTOP

If you get bored with the standard desktop colors, NT includes a number of preformatted color schemes that are much more exciting (at least, as exciting as a color scheme can get). You can even fiddle with the preformatted schemes and customize them completely to your own bizarre tastes. In addition, you can make other changes to NT's desktop appearance, too—such as changing the fonts that appear in the title bar and adjusting the *resolution,* or crispness, of your monitor's display.

To make these changes, right-click the desktop and choose the Properties command. Then, when NT displays the Display Properties dialog box, click on the Appearance tab, which is shown in Figure 10.2.

The top part of the dialog box contains a figure, which names all the components of the desktop. This figure also reflects any changes that you make as you go. The bottom half of the dialog box provides the controls for changing either an entire color scheme or any individual element on the desktop.

Changing the Color Scheme

NT comes with a bunch of different color schemes. Each of these color schemes uses a palette of (supposedly) compatible colors for the different elements of the NT desktop—including the desktop background, the different parts of windows, and the various other pieces of the NT user interface.

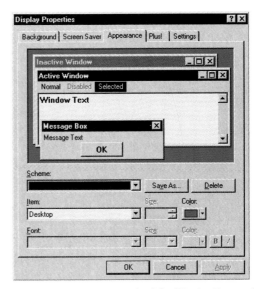

Figure 10.2 You use the Appearance tab of the Display Properties dialog box to adjust the way your desktop and windows look

You don't have to stick with the default color scheme. You can easily change the color scheme. If you're still in the Appearance tab of the Display Properties dialog box, select the Scheme drop-down list box:

NT shows you a list of the preformatted color schemes. All you do is click on a scheme that looks interesting. Note that the sample figure at the top of the dialog box shows you what the change looks like.

Changing Individual Elements of the Color Scheme

If you don't like some individual element of an existing color scheme, you can change it. First, display the Appearance tab of the Display Properties dialog box. Then click the part of the desktop that you want to change. The Item drop-down list box changes to show the element you clicked, and, if appropriate, the Font drop-down list box shows the current setting, too. By changing these settings, you can control every aspect of any element on the desktop. As you change the settings, the sample figure at the top of the dialog box reflects your changes.

Once your desktop is just the way you like it, click the Save As button to see the following dialog box:

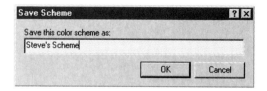

When NT asks you to name your new settings, provide a name and click OK.

Adjusting the Desktop Background

You can also display the Display Properties dialog box by opening the Control Panel folder and then double-clicking on the Display tool.

Sometimes, just changing the color of the desktop isn't enough. Your heart yearns for change, to break free from all the other lives of quiet desperation. Fear not—you can also add patterns and textures to the desktop. To make this change, you'll again need to use the Display Properties dialog box, such as by right-clicking the desktop and choosing the Properties command. When NT displays the Display Properties dialog box, click the Background tab.

As you can see in Figure 10.3, NT gives you two boxes to work with: Pattern and Wallpaper. The Pattern list box allows you to place a screen on top of the desktop background to add texture, while the Wallpaper box actually changes the picture or drawing that is displayed on top of the pattern.

**habits &
strategies**

*If you use a wallpaper that has
a lot of different colors or
designs, set the Pattern to
[None], and vice versa.
Combining the two can bring
about some very odd (and
distracting) results.*

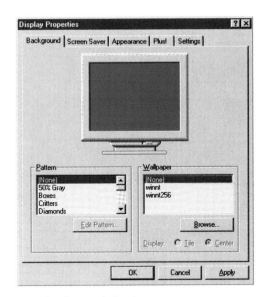

Figure 10.3 Doing a background check

Changing the Patterns

If you want to see what a pattern looks like up close, pick one, then click
the Edit Pattern button. NT opens the Pattern Editor dialog box:

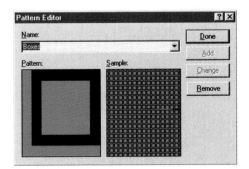

Using the Pattern Editor dialog box, you can change the desktop
background pattern. By clicking individual squares in the illustration on
the left, you turn individual picture elements, or *pixels,* on and off. NT
shows you how your pattern looks in the illustration on the right. If you
like your changes, give the pattern a name (using the Name box) and
click Done.

The Browse button in the Wallpaper box displays the common Open dialog box, which you can use to specify a graphic image file other than one in NT's default directory.

Wallpapering a Desktop

As mentioned earlier, the Background tab's Wallpaper setting allows you to use a picture for your desktop. There are two ways to arrange the pictures, which correspond to the Display option buttons at the bottom of the Wallpaper box: Tile and Center.

The Tile option button repeats the picture over and over again on the desktop, allowing you to fill the desktop with a small image. If you choose an image from the scroll box, the actual picture is very small, maybe one-fiftieth of the desktop space.

The Center option uses the picture just once and places it right in the middle of the desktop. Needless to say, the picture you choose must be large enough to use in this manner.

As before, the illustration above the boxes changes so that you can examine the impact of your choices.

CUSTOMIZING YOUR MENUS

With NT, you use the Start menu as one of the primary tools for starting programs and opening documents. (The Windows desktop and the My Computer program, I would say, are the two other main tools.) For this reason, NT makes it easy to customize the Start menu and its submenus as well as the task bar.

Customizing the Task Bar

You can make two changes to the task bar: you can change its location on the screen, and you can change its appearance. Changing the task bar location is easy. Simply drag it to where you want it to be. You can place the task bar along any of the four edges of the NT desktop. If you drag it someplace crazy and decide you don't like the new location, just drag the task bar back to its original location.

To make changes to the task bar's appearance, you need to display the Taskbar Properties dialog box. To do this, click the Start button. Then choose the Settings | Taskbar command. When you do this, NT displays the Taskbar Properties dialog box shown in Figure 10.4. Click on the Taskbar Options tab, if it is not already showing.

The Taskbar Options tab gives you four check boxes for customizing the menus. The Always on top option tells NT that nothing is

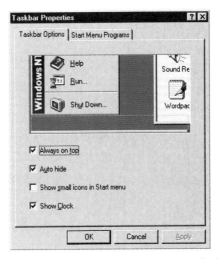

Figure 10.4 The Taskbar Properties dialog box, with the Taskbar Options tab showing

If you place the mouse cursor over the clock and wait a second, it will show the system date.

allowed to cover the task bar. No matter how many dialog boxes or windows you open, the task bar will be on top of the pile. The Auto hide option makes the task bar appear only when thc cursor is moved to where the task bar is located. The Show small icons in Start menu option tells NT to use smaller icons in the Start menu so that more programs will fit on the screen. Finally, the Show Clock option places a digital clock on the right side of the task bar (later in this chapter, I'll show you how to set the time on your system clock).

Customizing the Start Menu

NT gives you a bunch of different choices for customizing the Start menu. You can put programs you work with most often on the Start menu, for example, or on the Programs menu. You can organize similar programs together on submenus. You can even place documents on menus—perhaps grouping the documents by category—so you can then open these documents (and start the associated programs) simply by choosing a command.

Okay, I admit it. These changes may not seem all that exciting. But you know what? They can result in real productivity gains by saving you time and by simplifying your computing environment. So I want to quickly explain how you make these customizations.

CAUTION

Unless you set the Taskbar Options to show the small icons, you quickly run out of space on the Start menu if you add menu items.

Adding a Shortcut to the Opening Start Menu

To add a program or document to the Start menu, start NT Explorer and open the folder that contains the program or document you want to add. Then, drag the program or document's icon to the Start button. That's it. Now, when you press Start, the program or document is on the menu. Neat and easy.

Adding a Shortcut to a Submenu

If you want to place a shortcut in a submenu, you do slightly more work. Open the Taskbar Options dialog box by clicking the Start button and then choosing the Settings | Taskbar command. When NT displays the Taskbar Properties dialog box, click on the Start Menu Programs tab (see Figure 10.5).

Click the Add button. When you do, NT displays the Create Shortcut dialog box. It asks you where the program or document you're trying to add is located. You either type the full file and path name into the text box provided or click the Browse command button to open the common Browse dialog box, which works like the My Computer program and lets you hunt around your hard disk for the program file or document file you want.

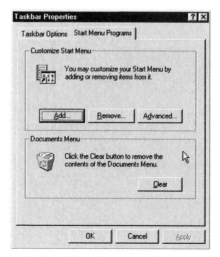

Figure 10.5 You use the Start Menu Programs tab to customize the Start menu

Once you identify the program or document you want to add to the Start menu or one of its submenus, you click Next. NT displays another Create Shortcut dialog box that asks where you want to put the program or document. To make your decision, just select the Start menu or submenu from the tree diagram shown on this Create Shortcut dialog box.

When you finish indicating where you want the menu item placed, click Next again. NT displays the final Create Shortcut dialog box. It just asks what name you want to use for the new menu item. Type the name and click Finish.

Removing a Shortcut from the Start Menu

Removing a shortcut from the Start menu is even easier. To remove an item from the Start menu, display the Taskbar Properties dialog box as described earlier. Click the Start Menu Programs tab. Click the Remove button, then click on the folders until you find the item you want to delete, click the item, and then click Remove.

If you are comfortable with NT Explorer, you can use the Advanced button of the Start Menu Programs tab to more quickly add and remove items from the Start menu. The Advanced button, however, provides no hand-holding.

Clearing the Document Menu

As noted in Chapter 2, NT automatically keeps track of the last 15 documents you have opened and places them on the Document menu. When you choose a document from here, NT automatically opens the proper program, then loads the document you have chosen.

To clear the list of documents, display the Start Menu Programs tab of the Taskbar Properties dialog box, and click the Clear button.

CUSTOMIZING NT EXPLORER AND MY COMPUTER

You can customize the way both the My Computer program and the NT Explorer program look and the way they organize the information contained within their windows. I'm going to describe here how all this works in the context of NT Explorer, but everything I say about NT Explorer also applies to My Computer.

habits & strategies

If there are programs you always turn on or documents you want to open each time you log on to NT, place a shortcut for them in the Start Up folder of the Programs menu. NT automatically starts any programs and opens any documents in this folder.

Let's get started. In Figure 10.6, the NT Explorer window shows the usual folder and file mishmash: different types of files, changed at different times, of different sizes. A real mess, if one is honest. Fortunately, changing the way NT Explorer displays and sorts this information can make working with this information much easier.

Adjusting the View

On the right side of the toolbar are four buttons that are often sadly neglected:

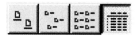

These buttons tell Explorer how to display the file information in the directory. From left to right, the four views are Large Icons, Small Icons, List, and Details.

Large Icons provide a view similar to the old Windows 3.1 application group windows. I think this view is awfully clumsy and unwieldy

**habits &
strategies**

If the toolbar isn't showing when you open NT Explorer, choose the View | Toolbar command.

Figure 10.6 A typical NT Explorer screen

for working with files. If readability is an issue for you, however, this is the best view to work with. Following are examples of a Large Icons view:

The Small Icons view is basically the same as Large Icons, but it uses the smaller version of the icons, so it is able to list the files in horizontal rows:

List takes the Small Icons view and places it in column form. Maybe accountants feel more comfortable with information in columns—I don't know. Following are examples of the List view:

Details takes the List view but adds a bunch of information: the file's name, size, type, and the last modification date:

Bubbles.bmp	3KB	Bitmap Image	7/11/95 9:50 AM
Calc.exe	58KB	Application	7/11/95 9:50 AM
Carved Stone.bmp	1KB	Bitmap Image	7/11/95 9:50 AM
Ccard232.exe	186KB	Application	7/20/95 12:00 AM

This is my favorite view, and not just because I tend to overcollect information (in spite of the boxes of old magazines in the garage). When you use this view, an extra row of buttons appears across the top of the file list:

When you press any of these buttons, NT sorts all of the files according to that criteria. This has literally saved me hours of unnecessary searching for that legendary Elusive File, which I always know is in the folder *somewhere*.

Specifying the Level of File Information

If you choose the View | Options command, NT displays the Options dialog box (see Figure 10.7). It lets you specify which folders and files you want to see and what file information you want to view. This dialog box also lets you tell NT that you want it to identify compressed files and folders using an alternate color.

If you mark the Hide files of these types option button, for example, NT basically doesn't display the program files that make up the operating system. (Usually this is what you want.)

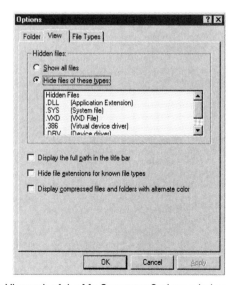

Figure 10.7 The View tab of the My Computer Options window

The three check boxes also affect the way files are displayed. The Display the full path in the title bar check box, for example, tells NT to display the entire path of the directory you're looking at in the title bar of the window. The Hide file extensions for known file types check box tells NT to hide the file name extensions that have been reserved by any program. Finally, the Display compressed files and folders with alternate color check box tells NT to flag any compressed files and folders by displaying them in a different color. (Chapter 11 talks about how you compress files.)

ADDING AND REMOVING PROGRAMS

NT provides a special Control Panel tool, which you use for installing new software programs. You'll also use this same tool for removing software programs you no longer need. This tool, called the Add/Remove Programs tool, does two things. It adds a command to the Start menu for the newly installed program, and it identifies for NT which documents belong to the program. (NT needs to know which documents belong to which programs so it knows which program to start when you tell it to open some document.)

Adding a Program

To install, or add, a new program, start the Add/Remove Programs tool. To do this, click the Start button. Choose the Settings | Control Panel command. Then, when NT displays the Control Panel folder, double-click the Add/Remove Programs tool, shown here:

Add/Remove
Programs

When NT starts the Add/Remove Programs Properties dialog box, click the Install/Uninstall tab if it isn't already showing. The Install/Uninstall tab is shown in Figure 10.8. Click the Install button. Then, when NT asks, verify that the first install diskette or CD-ROM is inserted in the appropriate drive and click Next.

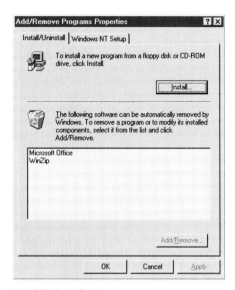

Figure 10.8 The Install/Uninstall tab

NT looks at the floppy disk or CD-ROM disk for an installation program. When it finds one, it asks you to confirm the install program, and then you click Finish. NT starts the installation program. From this point forward, all you have to do is follow the on-screen instructions. (If the Add/Remove Programs tool doesn't find an installation program, it asks you where the program you want to install is located.)

Removing a Program

The bottom half of the dialog box shown in Figure 10.8 lists the programs that NT can automatically remove, or uninstall. To remove any of these programs, just click on the name of the program you wish to remove. Then click the Add/Remove button. After confirming that you want to delete the program, NT looks for the information it needs to delete the program, then it removes the program. It's really quite easy.

CHANGING REGIONAL SETTINGS

As you move around the world, people make all sorts of changes in the way they work—and, as a result, in the way they use their computers. They punctuate numbers, dates, and times differently, for example. They often use different languages. And they transact business in different currencies (and sometimes even multiple currencies).

NT's designers thought of all these differences, of course. And so there's a special Control Panel tool—the Regional Settings tool—that lets you adjust the way NT works for local conditions and conventions. To use the Regional Settings tool, click Start. Choose the Settings | Control Panel command. And then double-click the Regional Settings tool. NT then displays the Regional Settings Properties dialog box (see Figure 10.9).

The Regional Settings tab lets you choose which language NT and other programs should use. This is the place to begin, because changing this setting will probably automatically set all of the other tabs properly. Since you already know how to operate a drop-down list box, I won't explain it here. I will mention, however, that I'm particularly enamored of the way the designers have allowed for different dialects of languages in this setting. It's an education in itself.

After changing the language shown on the Regional Settings tab, you should click each of the other tabs on the Regional Settings

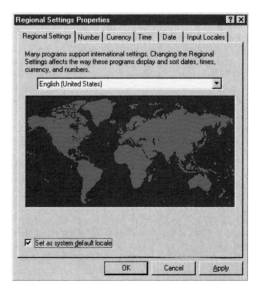

Figure 10.9 The Regional Settings tool lets you change the language that NT uses and a bunch of other stuff as well

Properties dialog box and review their settings. Click the Number tab, for example, and make sure that NT will punctuate numbers in the way you want. Click the Currency tab and make sure that NT will denominate currency amounts using the appropriate monetary units and currency symbols. Do the same thing for the Time, Date, and Input Locales tabs, too.

If you change the setting, NT asks whether you want to restart the computer to make the change permanent or not. If you're just trying it out, click No and then take a look at the other tabs to see how the formats of other countries differ from ours (just remember to change it back before closing the window). Otherwise, click Yes.

ADJUSTING YOUR SYSTEM DATE AND TIME

You computer's internal system clock does a great job of keeping track of the correct date and time, once you have it set. It automatically adjusts for leap years and daylight savings time—all those little things that are annoying to have to remember (especially when you're busy resetting every clock you own).

Nevertheless, you may still need to adjust the date or time if something goes haywire. So NT provides a Date/Time tool that you can use for just this purpose. To adjust the date or time, open the Control Panel by clicking the Start button and choosing the Settings | Control Panel command. Double-click the Date/Time tool. When the Date/Time Properties window opens, click on the Time Zone tab to see a cool map of the world, divided according to time zones (see Figure 10.10).

Use the drop-down list box above the map to set the correct time zone for your location.

Now click on the Date & Time tab, and the map is replaced by Figure 10.11.

There are a few different ways to change the settings. If you highlight the month drop-down box, you can type the first letter of the desired month. If there is more than one month beginning with that letter, NT will cycle to the next month with that letter (January, June, and July, for instance, if you type the letter J).

Be sure the check box under the map is checked, so the system will automatically keep track of daylight savings time.

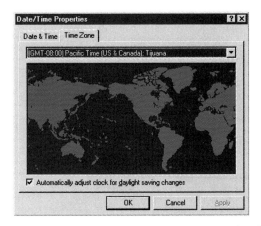

Figure 10.10 The Time Zone map lets you select a time zone by clicking a map of the world

To change the date, you can either highlight the date and type in the number, or just click on the number in the calendar. Either option works fine.

Unfortunately, you can't drag the clock's hands around to change the time. You can highlight the part of the time you want to change, however, and then either type in the correct setting or use the scroll buttons to the right of the box to change it.

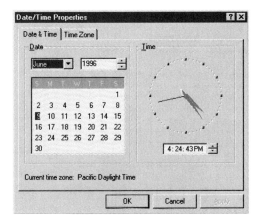

Figure 10.11 The Date & Time tab lets you adjust the system date and time

CHANGING THE KEYBOARD AND MOUSE SETTINGS

People often don't pay enough attention to the keyboard and mouse. Minor changes to the ways that either of these input devices work, however, can make your work much easier.

I'm going to give you the most important and useful keyboard and mouse customization techniques in the paragraphs that follow. But if you have more time, you might want to explore some of the other techniques that NT makes available.

Adjusting Your Keyboard Keys

If you change keyboards, you will need to make sure NT has the proper settings. Open the Control Panel by clicking the Start button and choosing the Settings | Control Panel command. Double-click on the Keyboard tool, and then click on the Speed tab for the controls shown in Figure 10.12. (You may need the original program disks to change the settings.) The Speed tab of the Keyboard Properties dialog box allows you to adjust the cursor blink rate and how the keyboard repeats characters if a key is held down.

Click on the Input Locales tab to see one of the most thoughtful ideas I've seen. If you work in more than one language or if you are one of those special people who prefer typing on a Dvorak keyboard, NT allows you to change your keyboard layout. NT enables you to set up

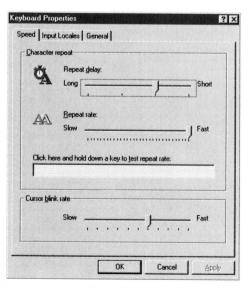

Figure 10.12 Use the Keyboard Properties dialog box to customize the way your keyboard works

definition

Dvorak keyboard: A special keyboard originally designed for faster typing by placing the most used keys in the most accessible positions. It never quite caught on.

your keyboard to handle two or more layouts, then lets you switch between each layout as you type.

Adjusting the Way Your Mouse Works

NT allows you to easily reverse the mouse buttons to make it easier for left-handed users. Open the Control Panel by clicking the Start button and choosing the Settings | Control Panel command. Double-click on the Mouse tool to open the Mouse Properties dialog box, then click the Buttons tab if it isn't already showing. The Buttons tab is shown in Figure 10.13. Select the Button configuration option button you want.

You can also set how fast you have to double-click before NT understands you. To do this, drag the Double-click speed slider button. Then, test your change by double-clicking in the test area.

The Motion tab of the Mouse Properties dialog box also provides several handy mouse adjustments (see Figure 10.14). If, for example, you have a small desk and not much room to move the mouse around, you want to be able to get the pointer across the screen with a minimum of movement. It would be to your advantage, therefore, to set the pointer speed to a faster setting. If, on the other hand, you do work that

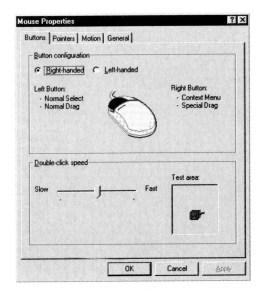

Figure 10.13 Adjusting the mouse for southpaws

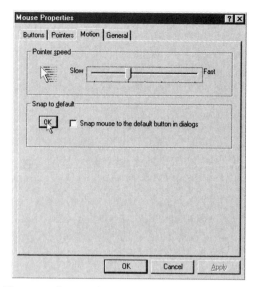

Figure 10.14 Mouse motion mania

requires more precise mousing—say, CAD/CAM work or graphics design—then a slower setting would allow you more control over your mouse positioning.

If you use your mouse to click dialog box command buttons rather than pressing ENTER all the time, then the Snap to default setting might interest you. If you check this box, NT automatically moves the cursor to the default button whenever an appropriate dialog box or window opens. The *default button* is the one that is highlighted whenever you are given a choice—usually the OK button.

CHANGING NT SOUNDS

Multimedia computers have the ability to handle many different sounds because they have special hardware, such as sound cards and speakers. If you are one of these lucky people, you can change the default NT sounds and save these changes as a personal sound scheme. You associate sounds in NT with events, such as opening a new program. I won't go into too much detail here, because it doesn't really do that much for productivity. It does, however, make your computer a lot more fun.

If you really want to be a sound hound, you can obtain many sound clips from Internet newsgroups and World Wide Web sites.

To make these changes, open the Control Panel by clicking the Start button and choosing the Settings | Control Panel command. Double-click on the Sounds tool. When NT displays the Sounds Properties dialog box (see Figure 10.15), highlight the event you want to change by clicking on it. Then choose the sound you want from the Name box. If your system is already set up for sound, the buttons to the right of the Preview box can be used to preview the sound, so you can make sure it doesn't annoy all your officemates. Once you set a sound for one event, click on another event to change the sound for it.

When you have all the sounds just the way you want them, click the Save As button and give it a name.

ON FROM HERE

There's only one chapter left in this book, which talks about how you can review NT's performance and fine-tune the way it runs. Once you've used the information in this chapter to customize NT the way you want, consider taking the time to review Chapter 11. It truly will complete your NT education.

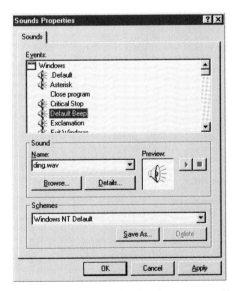

Figure 10.15 The Sounds Properties dialog box lets you specify which sounds NT uses

CHAPTER 11

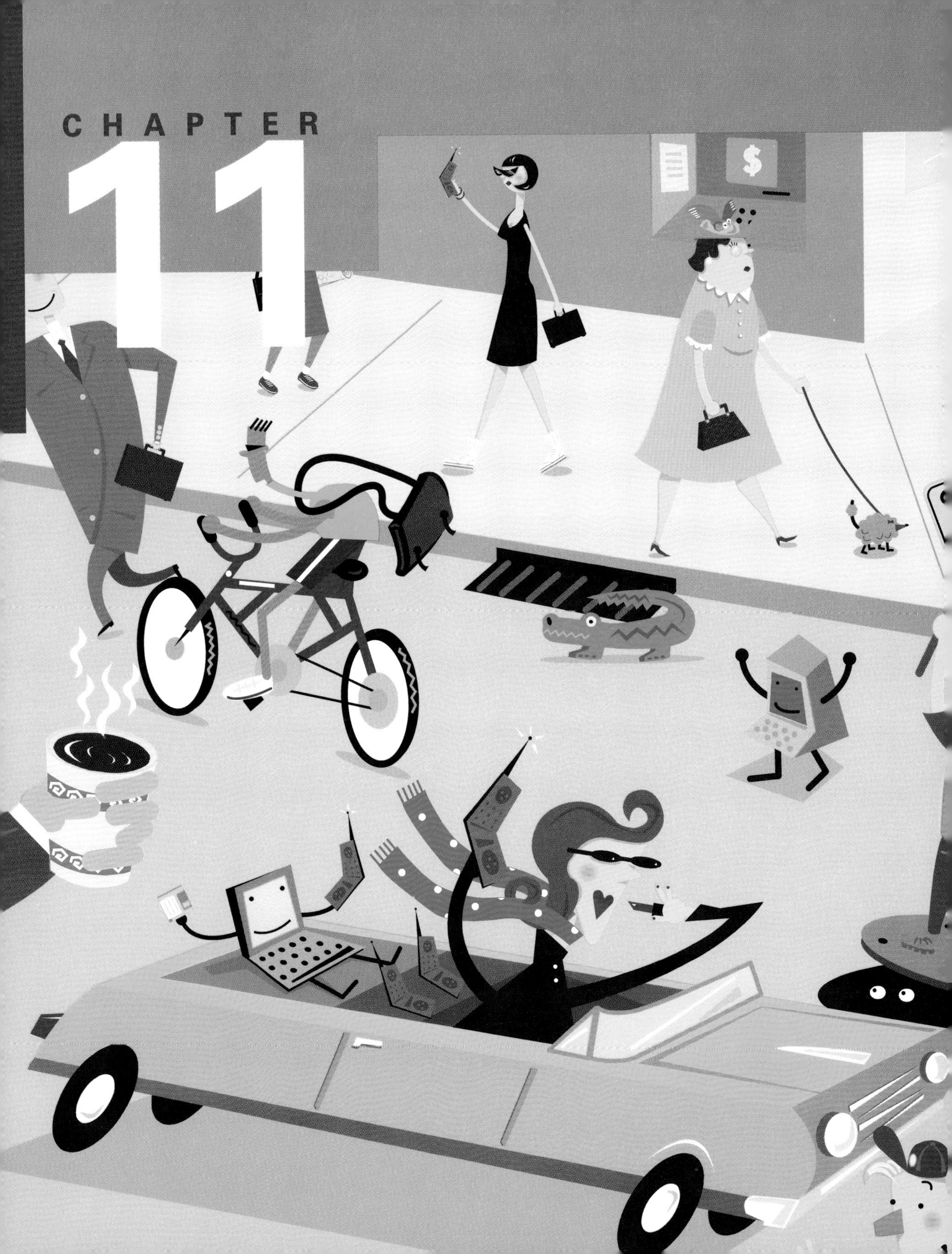

Fine-Tuning NT

INCLUDES

- Using the Task Manager

- Compressing and uncompressing disks

- Using the System tool

FAST FORWARD

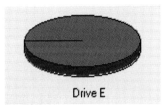

START TASK MANAGER ➤ *pp. 208-209*

Press CTRL-ALT-DEL so that NT displays the Windows NT Security dialog box. Then click the Task Manager command button.

MANAGE APPLICATION PROGRAMS ➤ *pp. 209-210*

Use the Task Manager's Applications tab to review the programs, or applications, you've started. To terminate an unresponsive application, click it and then click the End Task command button.

ADJUST SYSTEM PROCESS PRIORITIES ➤ *pp. 210-212*

The Task Manager's Processes tab describes everything the operating system is doing by listing each process and its resource usage. To change the priority of a process, right-click the process to display a shortcut menu. Choose the Set Priority command so that Task Manager displays the Set Priority submenu. Then choose one of the Set Priority submenu commands.

REVIEW RESOURCE USAGE ➤ *pp. 212-213*

Use the Task Manager's Performance tab to research how hard your CPU works and how much memory your programs and the NT operating system use.

COMPRESS A DISK ➤ *pp. 213-214*

Start NT Explorer. When the NT Explorer window opens, right-click on the disk you want to compress. Select Properties, and when NT displays the Properties dialog box, click the General tab and then mark the Compress check box.

Used space:

Free space:

UNCOMPRESS A DISK ➤ *pp. 214-215*

Start NT Explorer. When the NT Explorer window opens, right-click on the disk you want to uncompress. Select Properties, and when NT displays the Properties dialog box, click the General tab and then mark the Uncompress check box.

System

USE THE SYSTEM TOOL TO ADJUST FOREGROUND PROGRAM PERFORMANCE ➤ *p. 215*

Display the Control Panel folder and double-click the System tool. When the System Properties dialog box appears, click the Performance tab and use the Application Performance slider button to adjust the resources devoted to the program you're running in the foreground program window.

You're not a technical guru. And you're not interested in becoming one. I know that. But even so, you'll benefit by knowing how to review and fine-tune the way NT operates. So that's what this chapter does. It explains how you work with the NT Task Manager to explore how much work your computer is really performing and to apportion your computer's resources among multiple programs. This chapter explains how to stretch your disk space by using NT's disk compression feature. And the chapter describes how you can use the Control Panel's System tool to adjust the performance of your foreground program.

USING THE TASK MANAGER

NT comes with a task manager that essentially does three things. It lists the programs—NT calls them applications—that you've started. It describes which processes NT is running and how these processes are using up your computer's resources (I'll explain what processes are in a minute). And it reports how much of your CPU's horsepower and how much of your memory is getting used.

Starting Task Manager

To start the Task Manager, press CTRL-ALT-DEL so that NT displays the Windows NT Security dialog box:

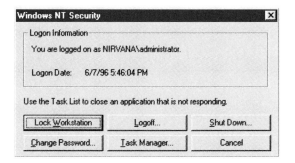

In this dialog box, click the Task Manager command button. NT starts Task Manager and displays its window, as shown in Figure 11.1.

Managing Application Programs

The Applications tab of the Task Manager dialog box—which is what's shown in Figure 11.1—just lists the programs that you've started. In Figure 11.1, you see only one program listed: the Microsoft Word program I'm using to write this chapter.

This "which applications are running" information isn't typically very useful—except in one special case. If something wacky happens to some program you're running and the program doesn't seem to respond to the keyboard or mouse, you can use the Applications tab to verify the program is still alive and well. See the Status column in Figure 11.1? Notice that the Microsoft Word application status shows as "Running." That's good. That means (at least from NT's perspective), everything is going smoothly. However, if the status shows as "Not responding," which is basically the other possibility, it means that from NT's perspective things aren't going smoothly—specifically that the application hasn't recently "checked in" with NT.

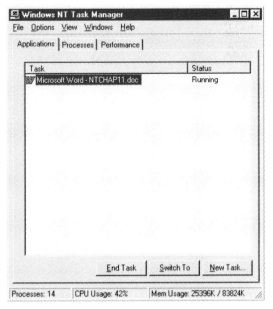

Figure 11.1 The Task Manager describes in precise detail what your computer is working on

When an application stops responding to NT and it stays unresponsive, you typically need to terminate the program. And you do this by clicking the application to select it and then clicking the End Task button, which appears near the bottom of the Task Manager window:

End Task

NT will display a warning message that tells you the unresponsive program may just be busy and asks if you want to wait. If you do want to wait, click the Wait command button. Otherwise, click End Task.

Adjusting System Process Priorities

The Task Manager's Processes tab, shown in Figure 11.2, describes everything the operating system is doing by listing each process and its resource usage. But before we get into the nitty-gritty details of the Processes tab, let me give you a bit of background on what processes are.

CAUTION

If you terminate a program that you've been using to create or edit a document, you lose whatever document changes you've made since the last time you saved the document. For this reason, wait a few minutes before ending a program that appears to be unresponsive.

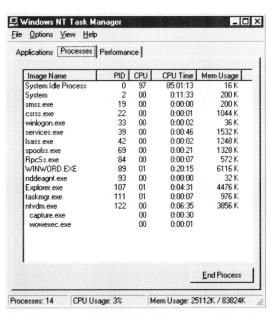

Figure 11.2 The Processes tab of the Task Manager window describes everything the operating system is doing

The term "process" sounds complicated, but it's really not. A *process* is essentially a program that you or the operating system starts. So if I'm banging out this chapter in Microsoft Word, WINWORD.EXE (which is the name of the Microsoft Word program) shows up as one of the processes listed on the Processes tab, because I started that program; if I've started other programs, they also show up. Not all processes get started by a user, however. The operating system also starts processes for doing operating system stuff. NT automatically starts the Explorer program, EXPLORER.EXE, for example. And there are a bunch of other processes that get started and are always running. WINLOGIN.EXE takes care of NT security stuff, for example. And SPOOLSS.EXE helps with printing, for another example. In short, each of the processes that the NT operating system runs also show up on the Processes tab.

Although you shouldn't fiddle with processes NT starts, you can change the priority of a process that you've started. For example, if you're running a program and you want its process to get a larger share of your computer's processing power, you can boost its priority. Or if you've got a program that should keep slogging away but really isn't very important, you can reduce its priority.

To change the priority of a process, right-click the process to display a shortcut menu. Choose the Set Priority command so that Task Manager displays the Set Priority submenu:

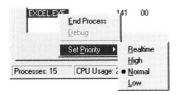

Then choose one of the Set Priority submenu commands: Low (to reduce the process's priority), High (to boost the process's priority), and Realtime (to really boost the process's priority). Note that the other Set Priority submenu command, Normal, resets the priority of some process you've previously adjusted back to its regular, normal priority, which is greater than Low but less than High.

You can also use the System tool, described later in this chapter, to direct NT to dynamically boost application performance based on whether a task runs in the foreground or the background.

You shouldn't reset process priorities willy-nilly, by the way. For this reason, NT warns you before it changes the priority of a process that noodling around with your process priorities may make your system unstable. To confirm that you want to change the priority, you click the Yes command button when NT displays a message box asking if you really want to change the process priority.

Reviewing Resource Usage

I think the Task Manager's most interesting and useful information appears on the Performance tab (see Figure 11.3). Interested in whether or not your computer's microprocessor (its CPU) is overtaxed? Start up all the programs you typically use and then take a look at the CPU Usage and CPU Usage History charts. They show you graphically how hard your CPU works as a percentage of its capacity.

Concerned that maybe you need to install more memory? Again, start up all of the programs you use, open a representative set of documents, and then look at the MEM Usage and Memory Usage History charts. If these two charts show that you're using all or most of your memory, you'll probably get a boost in performance by installing

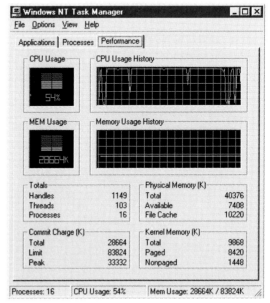

Figure 11.3 The Performance tab shows how much of your CPU's capacity and how much of your memory NT and your programs are using

more memory. If you're not using all of your memory (which is what Figure 11.3 shows, since I've got 40 megabytes of memory in my computer), then you know you don't need more memory.

USING NT'S DISK COMPRESSION

You can compress the files and folders stored on a disk that uses NT's file system, NTFS. When you do this, the files and folders you compress get scrunched by NT so that they take up less hard disk space.

Compressing a Disk

To compress a disk, start NT Explorer, such as by clicking the Start button and then choosing the Programs | Windows NT Explorer command. When the NT Explorer window opens, right-click on the disk you want to compress and select Properties so that NT displays the Properties dialog box as shown in Figure 11.4. If it doesn't already show, click the General tab.

habits & strategies

Some files, such as graphic images and word processing files, compress to a small percentage of their original size. Many files, however, including program files, don't shrink much when you compress them.

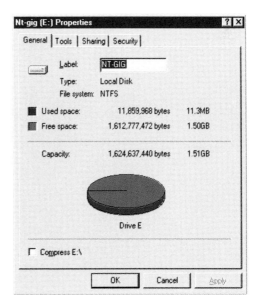

Figure 11.4 You use a disk's Properties dialog box to tell NT to compress the disk

To tell NT you want it to compress a disk, mark the Compress check box shown in the lower-left corner of the dialog box. Then click the Apply button. NT displays a message box indicating it will compress all of the files stored in the selected disk's root directory but not those stored in subfolders:

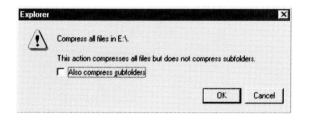

If you want to also compress subfolders—and you almost certainly do—mark the Also compress subfolders check box. Then click OK, and NT compresses the files.

Uncompressing a Disk

On a powerful computer—say a fast Pentium or a Pentium Pro—you should see no degradation in performance if you have NT compress your files. Note, however, that NT goes to quite a bit of work to scrunch files (as it saves them to the disk) and to unscrunch them (as it grabs them from the disk and passes them to a program). So, it's possible that you'll feel your computer slow down after you choose to compress a disk. If this happens, and speed is more important than free disk space, then you can uncompress a disk by following almost the same steps you used to originally compress the disk.

To uncompress a disk, start NT Explorer, such as by clicking the Start button and then choosing the Programs | Windows NT Explorer command. When the NT Explorer window opens, right-click on the disk you want to uncompress and select Properties. NT displays the same Properties dialog box shown in Figure 11.4, except that instead of a Compress check box, the dialog box will show an Uncompress check box.

To tell NT you want it to uncompress a previously compressed disk, mark the Uncompress check box and click the Apply button. NT next displays a message box that indicates it will uncompress all of the files stored in the selected disk's root directory but not those stored in subfolders. If you want to also uncompress subfolders, mark the Also uncompress subfolders check box. Then click OK, and NT uncompresses the files.

USING THE SYSTEM TOOL

Earlier in this chapter, I described how you can use the Task Manager to change the priority of processes. While the Task Manager gives you the most control over process priorities, the Control Panel's System tool provides an easier and usually more convenient way to change the way that your computer's resources are apportioned among those tasks you've started and that use the Normal priority. Unless you've changed a task's priority using the Task Manager, all the tasks you've started should still have the Normal priority.

To use the System tool, first display the Control Panel folder, such as by clicking Start and then choosing the Settings | Control Panel command. Then double-click the System tool, shown here:

When the System Properties dialog box appears (see Figure 11.5), click the Performance tab and use the Application Performance slider button to adjust the resources devoted to the program you're running in the foreground program window. To boost the performance of the foreground application, drag the slider button right. To boost the performance of any background applications, drag the slider button left. After you drag the slider button, click the Apply command button.

Foreground program window:

The program window that appears on top of all the other program windows. The program that appears in the foreground program window is the foreground application, and it gets a larger share of your computer's resources.

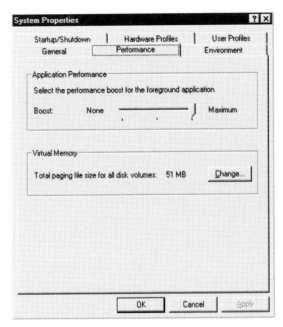

Figure 11.5 The System Properties dialog box lets you boost the performance of the foreground application at the expense of background applications

ON FROM HERE

This is the last chapter, but let me mention that this book does include several of appendixes: Appendix A, which talks about how you install Windows NT Workstation; Appendix B, which discusses in general terms how you set up a small network; Appendix C, which acts as an emergency guide to finding lost files; Appendix D, which is a discussion of Microsoft's BackOffice; and Appendix E, which is a table of MS-DOS and NT commands.

APPENDIX

Installing Windows NT Workstation

I'm going to level with you. I recommend you don't install Windows NT. Let someone else do it. And here's the way my logic goes. If you're installing Windows NT yourself, it's probably because you're either upgrading from another operating system (like MS-DOS and Windows 3.x) or because you're installing Windows NT on a brand-new computer that was really built and sold for use with Windows 95.

If you still want to install

Windows NT, it is explained (in

rough terms) in the "Installing

Windows NT Yourself" section.

Don't attempt to install Windows

NT for the first time, however,

until you read the next section,

"Getting Ready to Install

Windows NT."

The problem in both cases, however, is that you can't be sure that NT will work on your computer. And if you encounter even the slightest little glitch—say you're missing a driver program that NT needs to communicate with your CD drive or your sound card—then you're going to either (a) spend hours of time figuring this thing out on your own, or (b) you're just going to end up bringing the computer to Joe's Repair Shop anyway. So, I figure, you're a busy person. You've got a life. You don't need to be earning, like, $4 an hour learning how not to install NT.

Let me also say that if you do bring your computer to Joe's Repair Shop, it'll probably take Joe or one of the other guys about 30 minutes to install NT. You'll pay—I'm just guessing here—around $30 to $40 for the installation. But it'll be worth it, because Joe and the gang know all the booby traps, so they'll be able to avoid them. What's more, when Joe finds out that your "baseometer" adapter or "valvo-leter" card doesn't work because it's not on the Windows NT hardware compatibility list, Joe and the gang will probably be able to swap your incompatible device for a compatible device. (There aren't really baseo-meter adapters or valvoleter cards, by the way. I just made this stuff up.)

GETTING READY TO INSTALL WINDOWS NT

To prepare to install Windows NT, you really need to do three things:

1. Verify you've got enough free disk space (a minimum of 118 megabytes for Intel microprocessor-based computers and a minimum of 149 megabytes for RISC-based computers like the Digital Equipment Alphas.)

You can get an updated Windows NT hardware compatibility list from Microsoft's Web site at http://www.microsoft.com.

If you previously used Windows 95 or MS-DOS as your operating system, Windows NT keeps your old system intact. You'll still have the option of booting your computer using your last operating system—as long as your old operating system can read your hard disk.

2. Verify that the computer on which you want to install Windows NT is on the Windows NT hardware compatibility list.

3. Decide on either the FAT or NTFS file system.

Prerequisite number 1 is pretty straightforward. Either you have enough disk space or you don't. If you don't, you'll either have to clean up your existing disk or replace it with another, larger disk. But prerequisites 2 and 3 are bit more involved. So I want to talk about both of them for just a few sentences.

Let's begin with the awkward issue first: the old hardware compatibility problem. Windows NT, for all of its wonderful features, doesn't run on all of the hardware that Windows 95 does. And this means that the very first thing you need to do is confirm that NT will run on your computer and all of its hardware. If you can't confirm this, you should assume that NT won't install completely or correctly on your computer. And you should assume this even if the guy who sold the computer swears to you that you'll have no trouble whatsoever.

To do this hardware compatibility research, you'll need to use the booklet entitled "Windows NT Workstation Hardware Compatibility List" or something like that. You should find this booklet inside the Windows NT Workstation packaging.

The other thing you need to do is select a file system. Most people get two choices. Choice number one is to use the old, MS-DOS FAT file system. Choice number two is to use the Windows NT NTFS file system. If you look through the documentation that comes with NT, you can read a lengthy discussion of each file system's pros and cons. And you may want to slog your way through this material.

From my perspective, however, the "which file system to use" decision boils down to a couple of key questions. Do you want to use NT's sophisticated file-level security features? Then you have to use NTFS, because only NTFS supports file-level security. Alternatively, do you still want to run another operating system on the computer—say MS-DOS, OS/2, or Windows 95? Then you have to use FAT, because these other operating systems can't read NTFS disks.

If you want to use NT's file-level security features *and* to use another operating system occasionally, then you need to have or install two hard disks in your computer (and then use one as your FAT disk

CAUTION

Although NT lets you boot from either your old or new operating systems, you probably shouldn't do this if your old system is Windows 95. Windows 95 fiddles with your computer and its components when it starts, which can cause problems for NT the next time it starts.

habits & strategies

If you're going to install Windows NT yourself, you should have already completed the preperation described in the previous chapter section.

and the other as your NTFS disk). Or, you need to decide which is more important: the security of NTFS or compatibility with another operating system.

If you're not sure what to decide here, take a few days to think about it. The reason is that the NT installation program gives you the choice of converting FAT disks to NTFS disks when you install NT. And that's a big advantage if you want to use NTFS on existing disks. If you tell the NT installation program that it shouldn't convert your existing FAT disks, there's no easy way to make this change later. You have to back up the disk, reformat it and partition it as an NTFS volume, and then restore the contents of the disk from tape or wherever.

Installing Windows NT Yourself

If you've decided to install Windows NT yourself, I want to congratulate you on your bravery. And inasmuch as you've decided to go this route, I'm not going to spend any more time trying to get you to change your mind. Let's just get through this thing in one piece.

The first thing you want to do is read the installation instructions that come with the Windows NT Workstation packaging. No, really, I mean it. There's about 40 pages or so to read. Take your time. You won't have difficulty understanding the material if you possess reasonable technical skills.

The next thing you want to do is collect detailed data on your computer system, including information about all the devices the computer uses, which IRQs these different devices use, and so forth. You may be able to get this information from your existing operating system. In Windows 95, for example, the Control Panel's System tool provides users with detailed information on their computer and its components. Or you may be able to get this information from the user documentation that came with your computer.

CAUTION

Special installation instructions apply when you install NT on a RISC-based computer or over a network. Refer to the user documentation for more information.

Once you've gotten this far—assuming you don't have a hardware compatibility problem—it isn't difficult to install Windows NT Workstation. Here's what you do.

1. Turn off your computer.
2. Insert the "Windows NT Setup Disk" into your A floppy drive. Or, if your computer's BIOS supports the El Torito CD-ROM format, insert the Windows NT Workstation 4.0 CD into the CD drive.
3. Turn on your computer. Follow the on-screen instructions. Religiously.

Getting Set up After You've Installed Windows NT

After you've installed Windows NT, you can begin using it. You will, however, need to do three more things. You may need to set up user accounts so people can log on to NT and begin using its horsepower; Chapter 6 describes how you do this. And you'll probably need to install some of your software (if you've been using the Microsoft Office for Windows 95 software, for example, you'll need to reinstall it to use it with Windows NT); Chapter 10 describes how you do this. And if you're connecting to a network, the network administrator will also need to set up an account for your computer.

APPENDIX

B

Setting up a Small Windows NT Network

A few years ago now, I had a cathartic experience. A young Microsoft programmer/millionaire visited my office and saw that we were using the Windows for Workgroups 3.11 software as the basis of a pretty rinky-dink, small network. He then pulled me aside and let me know that I was a fool to not be using a real 32-bit network operating system, like Windows NT or one of the other network operating systems.

I'm going to assume that either you've read Chapter 1 or know the information it covers. If you encounter terms you don't know, consider flipping back to Chapter 1.

The gist of his analysis was this: As long as you don't get too crazy and try to create some multiple-domain, 1,000-seat network, it's just not that tough to build an NT network. Even for people like you and me. You need a server or two or three to off-load the dirty work of running a network (for this, you use Windows NT Server). You'll need cabling and some network cards. And you'll need operating system software for the client computers—preferably Windows NT, but one can also easily use Windows 3.*x* or Windows 95.

I'm not saying, by the way, that setting up a small Windows NT network is something that any old idiot can do. You've got to want to do it. And you need some modicum of technical proficiency. But if you've been reading the earlier chapters of this book and you're getting the hang of NT, I think you can do it. I really do. So I want to tell you how you go about doing this.

GETTING READY

In order to connect your computers to the cabling that connects a network, you need a network adapter card. This card plugs into your computers' motherboards in the same manner that internal fax/modem cards plug into a motherboard.

You can't really go wrong in terms of buying the network card. Oh, I'm sure that some manufacturers' cards are slightly better than others. But if you buy a network card manufactured by somebody you've heard of before—Intel, 3Com, or somebody else like that—you're not going to go wrong. (You don't really need to know this, but what you're getting is a 10 Mbps 16-bit Ethernet adapter.)

The one thing that is important is that the network cards you get all need to be able to connect to the same type of cabling. For all practical purposes, you've got two choices for cabling: coaxial cable (which is like the cabling that the television cable company uses) and unshielded twisted pair, or UTP, cable (which is like the thin, flat-ish wire that the phone company uses to connect your telephone to the wall outlet).

If you choose UTP cabling, you actually need one other piece of hardware called a hub, or star, into which each of the UTP cables plug:

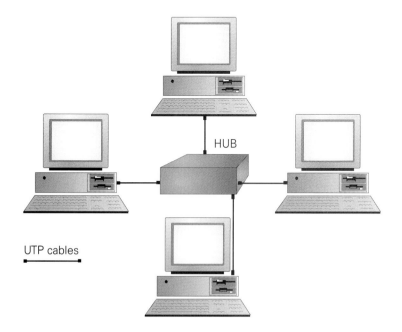

In comparison, with coaxial cabling, you just cable the individual computers together:

If you're setting up a small network—say less than a dozen computers—it doesn't really matter which cabling option you choose. Both have advantages. Both have disadvantages. If you're really serious about this, find a good computer salesperson or a local consultant and ask him or her to help you assess your situation.

Once you've got your network cards installed and you've got a bunch of cabling with which to connect your computers, you're ready to set up your server.

INSTALLING WINDOWS NT SERVER

Windows NT Server isn't any more difficult to install than Windows NT Workstation. (Appendix A pleads with you not to do this yourself, but it also tells you how). The only thing that's different about installing Windows NT Server is that a server can fulfill one of three roles: primary domain controller, backup domain controller, and member server. And you've got to identify which role you want a server to fulfill when you install the server software.

Let me explain. A Windows NT domain is a group of computers that use the same domain controller to authenticate users who log on to and computers that connect to the network. Each domain needs at least one computer—a *domain controller*—to check user names and computer names against a directory of users and computers that are authorized to do network stuff. When you install Windows NT Server, therefore, you need to specify whether the server you're setting up is a domain controller or not. If the server is a domain controller, you make this indication and provide the domain name. This is how you actually create the domain.

If the server isn't a domain controller, what you're setting up is a *member server*. This just means you're setting up a server that'll do server-type stuff (like printing, for example, or running server software). But it's not a server that will have the job of authenticating, or verifying, users and computers.

A network needs one primary domain controller and can have multiple backup domain controllers. But you probably won't need very many domain controllers (and may even want to live life on the edge and use only one domain controller), because each domain controller can manage, oh, maybe 2,000 users or computer accounts.

Any computers running Windows NT Server that aren't domain controllers are member servers. So—and this is the main point you need to take away from this—you need to know whether the computer on

habits & strategies

When you install Windows NT Server, you pick a networking protocol—the language that the network's computers use to talk to each other. For a small network, NetBEUI is fine.

which you or someone else is installing Windows NT Server is the primary domain controller, a backup domain controller, or just a member server. This may sound complicated, but let me say this another way. If the server is the first one you're setting up, it has to be the primary domain controller (since you need at least one of these). If the server is the second one you're setting up, it should probably be the backup domain controller (you don't want to lose your network just because, for example, the hard disk on your primary domain controller fails). And if you've already got the primary domain controller and backup domain controller set up and your network is a small one, the third and subsequent servers should be member servers, because they're not domain controllers. If this all makes sense to you, you understand how to install Windows NT Server (or at least how to give correct installation instructions to the technical support that installs Windows NT Server).

Once you've got your Windows NT Server computer set up and ready to go (and Windows NT Workstation or Windows 95 installed on all of the client computers), you're pretty much ready to start up the network. You cable everything together. A five-year-old can do this. Then, using the primary domain controller, you start the User Manager for Domains program to set up accounts for all of your users and all of the computers that will connect to the network.

ADMINISTERING A WINDOWS NT NETWORK

Administering a network takes more work than administering a stand-alone computer. It's not an unbearable burden. But you do need to plan for and schedule this work, which includes: backing up the network's data files; setting up new user and computer accounts; and installing service packs.

If you're going to be the one doing this, you'll richly benefit by taking a day or two of classes on Windows NT Server. Your local community college probably offers a whole slew of these. You'll also benefit by getting one or more of those thorough Windows NT Server reference books. You should also budget some money for technical support calls or service. If you encounter system error events, you'll probably need help resolving these problems. And that help will cost

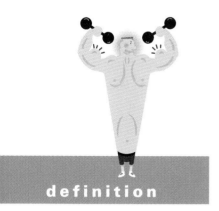

Chapter 6 describes how to use the User Manager program that comes with Windows NT Workstation, but the User Manager for Domains program works in the same basic way.

definition

Microsoft periodically releases an updated set of operating system files called a service pack *to fix bugs and other problems.*

habits & strategies

You may be able to get technical support from the company that sells you your computers. Note, too, that Microsoft Corporation offers numerous technical support plans for Windows NT network users.

you to the tune of about $200 per telephone call. You can also sometimes get technical support from local companies or consultants for lower prices.

SOME CLOSING COMMENTS

When I first started using personal computers more than a dozen years ago, the operating system and application software were pretty unfriendly. Getting a popular program like Lotus 1-2-3 to print required an undue amount of effort, for example. Configuring a serial printer—well, let's not even go down that road.

I don't want to scare you away from a Windows NT network if you're part of a small business or nonprofit organization, but things with NT are much the same way. An NT network represents a quantum leap in complexity compared to, say, a single, stand-alone personal computer running Windows 95 or an Apple Macintosh running the MacOS.

The thing you have to remember, however, is that a Windows NT network also delivers huge increases in productivity. Sure, it's a hassle and it's a bit scary to get started networking. But being able to easily share information with everybody you work with? Being able to work in a secure computing environment? Being able to share networking resources like super-fast printers and huge hard disk drives? Man, I tell you, it's all worth it.

APPENDIX C

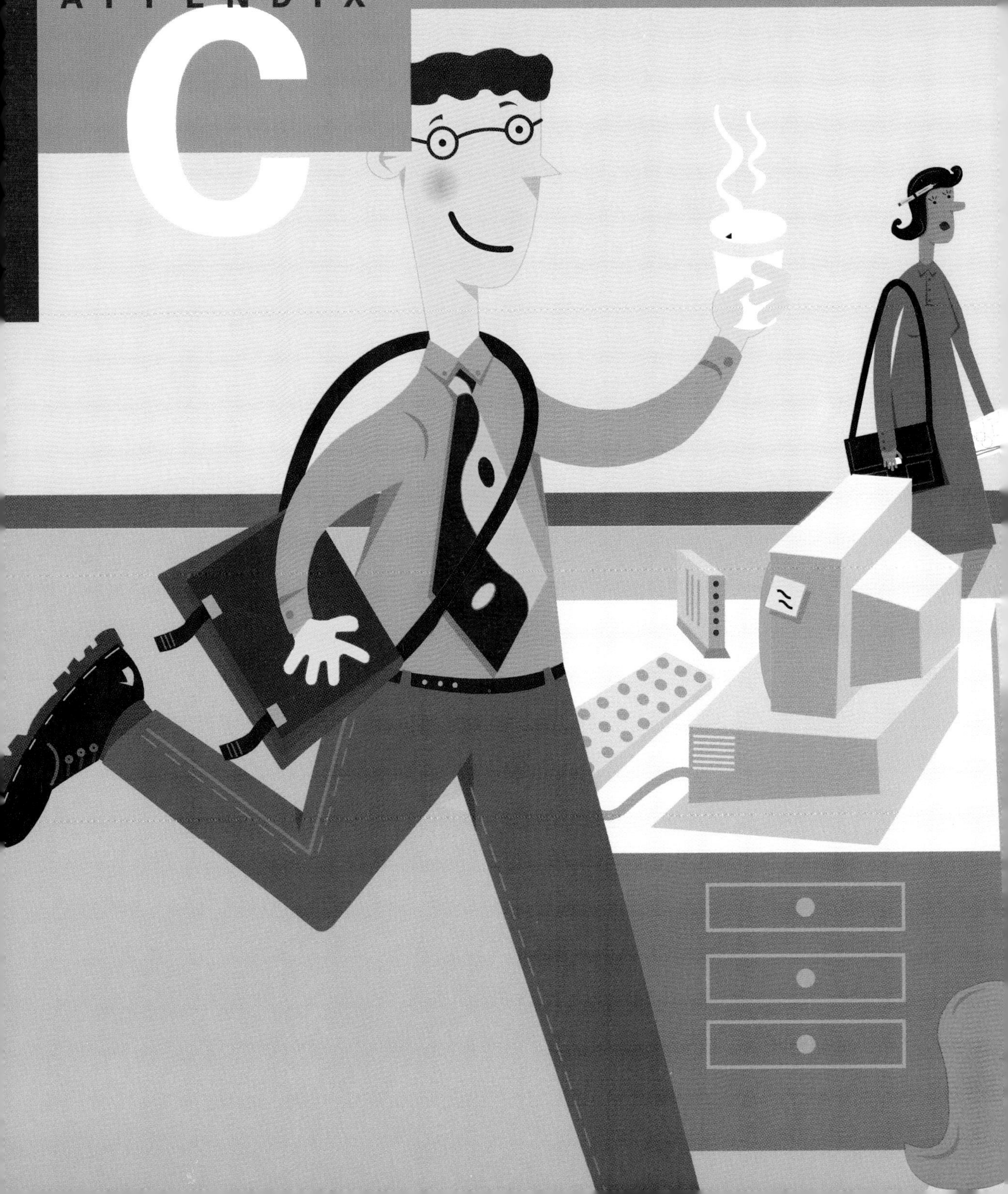

Emergency Search and Rescue

The Find command that NT supplies on its Start menu lets you search a network for a particular computer or search a hard disk for a particular file. Using Find isn't difficult, thankfully.

But there's a bit more to it than meets the eye. So this quick appendix explains how Find works and why you might use it. (By the way, you'll find it most easy to work with Find if you already understand how either the My Computer or NT Explorer programs work.)

FINDING MISSING COMPUTERS

You need to know a computer's name to map its network drives. But what do you do when you don't know the computer's name—or aren't sure you know it? Here's the practical answer: As long as you know a computer's name—or some portion of its name—you can use the Find command to locate the computer on a network. To do this, click the Start button and then choose Find | Computer. When NT displays the Find Computer window shown here, enter the name of the computer you want to locate in the Named text box.

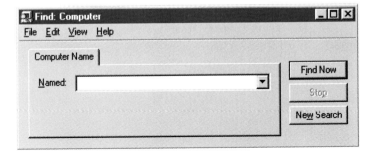

If you want to determine whether or not there's a computer named "Godzilla" connected to the network, for example, you could type **Godzilla**. Usually, however, you won't know a computer's complete name. (If you did, you wouldn't need to use Find.) So, what you'll usually do is enter part of a computer's name and then use wildcards to represent the parts of the computer that you don't know. You use the asterisk (*) character to represent any group of characters and the question mark (?) character to represent any single character. But let me explain.

Say that you want to find a computer (perhaps so you can map to its network drives) and that you know the computer's name starts with the letter "g." You can't remember, however, if the name is "Gonzo," "Gilgamesh," or something else like this. In this case, you enter **g*** in the Named text box. This tells NT to look for any computer names that start with the letter "g." If NT finds a computer with the name you entered, it displays the computer in a list box at the bottom of the window, shown here:

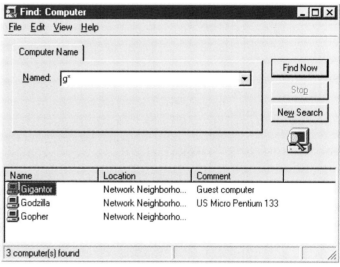

The Find Computer window's menus provide essentially the same set of commands as do the My Computer and NT Explorer windows.

You can continue to search for computers by entering new computer name descriptions into the Named box. When you click the Find Now button, NT adds any new computers it finds to the bottom of the list. If you want to start over, click the New Search button.

Once you find the computer you want (or once you find the computer you think you want), double-click its name in the list box. NT then opens a window that shows the shared folders available on the computer's disks. You work with this window the same way you work with My Computer windows or the NT Explorer windows. (Chapter 4 describes the My Computer program; Chapter 8 describes the NT Explorer program.)

FINDING LOST FILES AND FOLDERS

With today's gigantic disks, it's often easy to lose or misplace a file. And that's particularly true when you use multiple disks (say both local and network disks) to store your files. Fortunately, you can also use the Find command to locate lost files. To begin using the Find command in this way, click the Start button and then choose the Find | Find Files or Folders command. NT displays the Find All Files window, shown here:

To search for a particular type of file, include the file extension in the Named drop-down list box. For example, to search for Microsoft Word document files, use the .doc file extension.

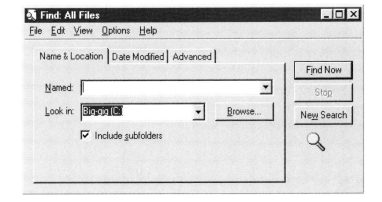

If you know the name of a file, but you just can't remember where it is, enter its name in the Named drop-down list box. Then use the Look In drop-down list box to specify which disk you want to search. If you want to search the entire disk, be sure you select the disk's root directory (in other words, the disk itself) and not one of its folders, and mark the Include Subfolders check box.

Once you've described in as precise detail as possible the file you want to locate, click Find Now to begin the search. In the status bar, NT tells you how many files it has found that meet your criteria. Below is the list box that NT adds to the Find All Files window once it has found one or more files like the one you're searching for.

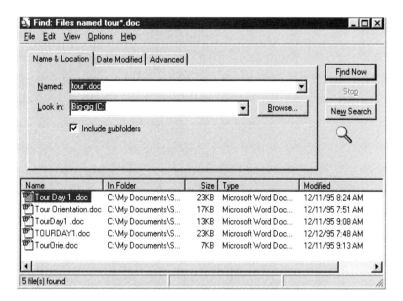

You don't need to search for files based on their names. You can also search based on file creation and modification dates and, in the case of document files (like Microsoft Word documents and Microsoft Excel workbooks), based on the contents of the files. For example, if you want to look for files that were created or modified during a particular month, display the Find All Files window as described earlier. Click the Date Modified tab so that NT displays the Date Modified buttons and boxes (as shown in the illustration that follows). Click the Find All Files Created Or Modified button to indicate you'll consider file creation and modification dates in your search. Then use the Between and During buttons to indicate which dates you want to search for. For example, to find files created during the month of May in 1996, you click the Between button and then enter 5/1/96 and 5/31/96 into the two text boxes provided. This makes sense, right? It's just a matter of clicking buttons and filling in boxes.

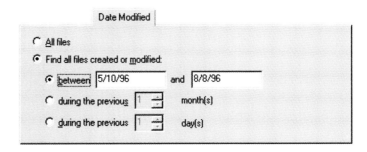

NT looks for files that match all of your search criteria: the Named criteria, the Date Modified criteria, and the Advanced criteria.

If you want to search for files based on their textual contents, display the Find All Files window as described earlier. Then click the Advanced tab so that NT displays the Advanced buttons and boxes:

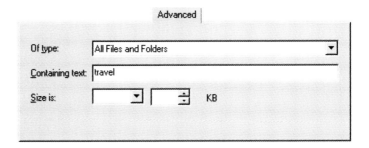

Use the Of Type drop-down list box to tell NT what you want it to search for. (If you activate this drop-down list box, NT displays a bunch of different choices—mostly corresponding to different file formats.) Use the Containing text box to indicate what text string you want to search for. For example, if you're looking for files that include the word "travel" someplace, enter **travel**. Optionally, use the Size boxes to specify that you're looking for files of at least or at most a certain size. Then, once you've described the search in these ways, click the Find Now button. And then go get yourself a cup of coffee because advanced searches take a long, long, long time. (If you want to stop a search that's already in progress, click the Stop button.) If you see the file you want, you just double-click it to open it.

habits & strategies

You can click the column

header buttons—Name,

In Folder, Size, Type, and

Modified—to sort the files

NT finds in ascending or

descending order by name,

folder, size, file extension, and

file modification date.

As NT finds files or folders that match your description, it displays them in a list box it adds to the bottom of the window. Here's an example of this.

Name	In Folder	Size	Type	Modified
Secret Business Pl...	C:\	56KB	Microsoft Excel Wor...	5/23/96 1:20 PM
NTchap10.doc	C:\	55KB	Microsoft Word Doc...	6/9/96 5:14 PM
windows.GID	C:\WINDOWS\HELP	232KB	GID File	5/17/96 3:41 PM
start.html	C:\Program Files\PL...	7KB	Internet Document (...	6/7/96 2:39 PM
ref.asp	C:\Program Files\PL...	8KB	ASP File	6/7/96 3:38 PM
maps (1).htm	C:\Program Files\PL...	4KB	Internet Document (...	6/7/96 3:38 PM

44 file(s) found

You now know most everything there is to know about the Find command—both the Find Computer version and the Find All Files version. But let me say just a couple more quick things. First, don't be afraid to experiment—especially with the Find All Files version of the command because it's more complicated to use. You can't do any damage just by using these two commands. And the more you work with both versions of the command, the more comfortable you'll become.

Second, remember that NT easily (and happily) multitasks. What this means in the case of the Find command is that you can start a Find command (such as one that looks for document files using the phrase, "For your eyes only") and then go off and work with some other program or document while the Find command runs. You can actually leave Find running for a few hours or even a few days.

APPENDIX D

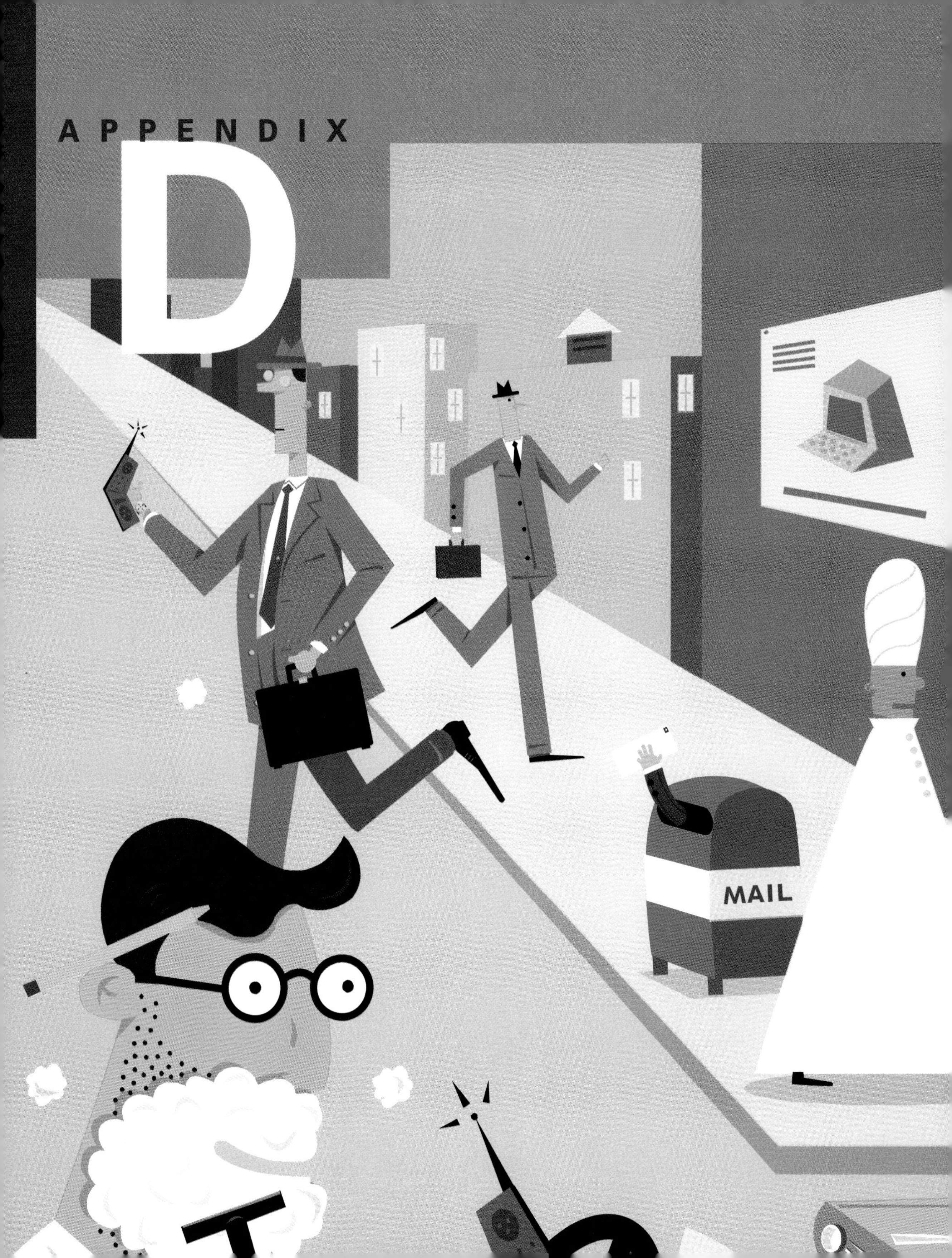

What's in Microsoft BackOffice

Throughout the earlier chapters and appendixes of this book, I've talked mostly about NT Workstation and then in a few places I've referred—often tangentially—to NT Server. I haven't talked about NT BackOffice, however.

So that's what I want to do here. My purpose in doing this, I should say, is not to turn you into some sort of network guru or systems consultant. I really only want to explain to you what BackOffice is so that you understand the term when you hear it—and, in the event you partici-pate in your organization's network planning—so that you know why BackOffice is important.

The Bird's-Eye View

In a nutshell, Microsoft BackOffice is really just a bunch of software products that Microsoft developed and that it sells for NT Client-Server networks. So, whenever you hear the term BackOffice, you can actually just think, "Oh yeah, that's just more NT Server stuff that Microsoft wants to sell."

Nevertheless, one shouldn't be too cynical about BackOffice because—and I'm not a big defender of Microsoft—BackOffice lets you do more with your NT network. For example, one piece of BackOffice provides your network with really cool super-powerful e-mail. Another part lets you build (or lets your consultants build) large, yet fast, database management systems. Still another part lets you create Internet and Intranet servers. And there are additional tools for network and work-station management as well as for connecting to a mainframe com-puter. To sum up, while NT Workstation and NT Server let you build a network and share resources, BackOffice supercharges your network.

What's in BackOffice

Not surprisingly, the BackOffice family of applications continues to grow over time. But at the time I'm writing this, BackOffice includes five products. In the paragraphs that follow, I'll briefly describe each of these products.

Microsoft Exchange Server 4.0

Microsoft Exchange Server lets you build a network electronic mail and group scheduling system. Exchange consists of two parts: a server component that you install on an NT member server, and a workstation component (or workstation components) that you install on each user's workstation. (Note that the version of Exchange that comes with NT amounts to a "lite" version of the real Exchange for NT Client.)

Microsoft SQL Server 6.5

SQL Server is a relational database management system that lets you manage and store large volumes of data. (SQL Server now includes a Web Assistant that makes it possible for you to distribute your company's data either within your company on your own Intranet, or to the general public on the World Wide Web.) If you wanted—or your organization wanted—to build a big, distributed database that, for example, collected and stored customer information and then made that information available to users running Windows 95 or Windows NT 4.0, you could use SQL Server. You would also, by the way, need client-workstation software running on users' desktop or laptop computers.

Microsoft Internet Information Server 1.0

Unless you've been in a cave for the last couple of years, you know the Internet is hot. White hot, in fact. The big money—at least from the software companies' point of view—comes from controlling or setting the industry and network standards. In this regard, Microsoft Corporation is actually playing catch-up (at least at this point) with Netscape Communications Corporation. So their Microsoft Internet Information Server—which is part of BackOffice and a good product—is free. What's it do? It lets you use an NT member server to publish your company's documents on the Internet or a private Intranet.

definitions

Member server: *A* member server *is a computer running the NT Server software that isn't a domain controller.*

Intranet: *A collection of web pages that are available only to a company's internal users.*

243

Microsoft Systems Management Server 1.1

Microsoft Systems Management Server lets network administrators better and more easily manage networks. With System Management Server, administrators can keep track of network hardware, manage the installation and usage of network software, diagnose and troubleshoot network problems, and monitor network performance. This piece of the BackOffice puzzle also provides a framework for a network helpdesk.

Microsoft SNA Server 2.11

The acronym SNA refers to Systems Network Architecture. Developed by IBM, SNA basically amounts to a set of rules that describes how one networks a bunch of different computers so everything works smoothly—or at least works. Microsoft SNA Server 2.11 applies the SNA design philosophy to connect desktop workstations and NT network servers with large mainframe computers.

E

CAUTION

Table of MS-DOS and NT Commands

As I mentioned in Chapter 8, NT comes with its own version of MS-DOS. Or, to be more precise, NT comes with an MS-DOS emulator that you can use to issue all the standard MS-DOS commands, as well as a handful of commands that really relate only to the NT operating system.

I can't provide exhaustive discussions about everything there is to know about each of these commands. But what I can do is describe the commands in a sentence or two and in a table. This will give you a way to quickly see what's possible.

If you have more questions about a particular command, start the MS-DOS command prompt (by clicking the Start button and then choosing Programs | Command Prompt) and then type the command **help** followed by the name of the command you want to know more about. For example, if you want to know more about the first command listed, type **help assoc.**

Command	What It Does
ASSOC	Tells which document file extensions are associated with which program file. For example, if you type **assoc .doc** at the command prompt, NT might display .doc=Word.Document.6 to inform you that the .doc file extension is associated with Microsoft Word version 6
AT	Tells NT to run a specific command at a specific time on a specific computer. The AT command is neat, no doubt, but expect to spend some time figuring out how it works
ATTRIB	Tells you what a file's attributes are and lets you change them
BACKUP	Backs up a file or set of files
BREAK	Turns on and off extended CTRL-C checking for the benefit of programmer types who are debugging some chunk of code. You *don't* need to worry about this one. Really.
CALL	Starts a batch program from a batch program. (*Batch programs* are just text files jam-packed with MS-DOS commands. When you start a batch program, NT just executes all the commands listed in the batch program's text file.)
CD	Tells you which directory is current and lets you change the current directory
CHCP	Lets you fool around with the active code page—something casual users never need to do

Command	What It Does
CHDIR	Equivalent to the CD command, CHDIR tells you which directory is current and lets you change the current directory
CHKDSK	Checks a disk for bad sectors and fragmentation and lets you fix most problems
CLS	Clears the command prompt window
CMD	Starts another instance of the NT's MS-DOS emulator
COLOR	Tells NT what colors you want to use for the console foreground and background
COMP	Compares the contents of files
CONVERT	Converts FAT volumes to NTFS volumes. Especially useful for people who blew off my advice in Appendix A
COPY	Copies one or more files to another disk or folder. For people who like to do things the hard way
DATE	Displays or sets your computer's internal system date
DEL	Deletes one or more files or folders
DIR	Lists the files and subfolders in a folder
DISKCOMP	Compares the files and folders of two floppy disks
DISKCOPY	Copies the files and folders of one floppy disk to another
DOSKEY	Starts a program that lets you edit previous MS-DOS commands, reuse commands, and even create macros
ECHO	Used in batch files, the ECHO command specifies what appears (or doesn't appear) on your screen
ENDLOCAL	Used in batch files, the ENDLOCAL command turns off localization of environment changes
ERASE	Essentially equivalent to the DEL command, the ERASE command deletes one or more files or folders
EXIT	Quits the MS-DOS command prompt and closes the command prompt window
FC	Compares files, displaying their differences
FIND	Searches for a text string in a document or set of documents, but still a poor substitute for the start menu's Find command (which I describe in Appendix C)
FINDSTR	Searches for strings in documents
FOR	Tells NT to run a particular command for each file within a set of files

Command	What It Does
FORMAT	Formats a floppy disk
FTYPE	Shows which file types are used for which file extension associations—and lets you make changes
GOTO	Used in batch programs, the GOTO command tells MS-DOS to jump to a particular line of a batch program
GRAFTABL	Lets NT's version of MS-DOS use an extended character set for graphics mode
HELP	Displays helpful information about most (but not all) of the MS-DOS commands
IF	Used in patch programs, the IF command tests conditional statements and controls program flow
KEYB	Localizes a keyboard for a specified language
LABEL	Labels a disk with a short, eight-character name
MD	Makes a folder or directory
MKDIR	Equivalent to the MD command, the MKDIR command makes a folder or directory
MODE	Lets you configure a device—such as a printer
MORE	Used with other commands, the MORE command tells NT to display command output one screen at a time
MOVE	Moves one or more files from one folder to another folder on the same disk
PATH	Displays or sets a path
PAUSE	Suspends execution of a batch program so you can display a message
POPD	Restores the current directory to the value previously saved by PUSHD command
PRINT	Prints the specified text file
PROMPT	Lets you fiddle with the NT command prompt window
PUSHD	Saves the current folder or directory (so you can later change back to it using the POPD command) and then changes the current folder or directory
RD	Removes a folder or directory
RECOVER	With luck, salvages readable information from a bad or defective disk

Command	What It Does
PUSHD	Saves the current folder or directory (so you can later change back to it using the POPD command) and then changes the current folder or directory
RD	Removes a folder or directory
RECOVER	With luck, salvages readable information from a bad or defective disk
REM	Used in batch programs and the CONFIG.SYS file, the REM command lets you add remarks and comments to batch files
REN	Renames a file or folder
RENAME	Equivalent to the REN command, RENAME renames a file or folder
REPLACE	Replaces files
RESTORE	Restores files previously backed up with the BACKUP command
RMDIR	Removes a folder or directory
SET	Shows and sets environment variables
SETLOCAL	Used in batch files, the SETLOCAL command turns on localization of environment changes
SHIFT	Used in batch files to fiddle with the position of replaceable parameters
SORT	Arranges input and then writes sorted information to the screen, a printer, or some other device
START	Starts a specified program or command
SUBST	Creates a virtual drive
TIME	Displays or sets your computer's internal system time
TITLE	Specifies what title NT should use for the command prompt window
TREE	Draws a tree to show the folder or directory structure of a disk
TYPE	Displays the text in a file
VER	Displays Windows NT version number information
VERIFY	Double-checks that NT correctly wrote your files to a disk
VOL	Displays a disk's volume label and serial number information
XCOPY	Copies files and folders or directory trees. In its time, a cool command, but now very passé

Index

A

Access Through Share Permissions dialog box, 105
Accessories, Windows NT, 115-133
Accessories menu, 21
Account groups, 95
    creating, 98-99
    editing, 99-100
    working with, 96-101
Account policies, setting, 100-101
Account Policy dialog box, 100
Accounts, 93-94
    creating, 97-98
    disabling vs. deleting, 98
    editing, 98
    working with, 96-101
Add Printer Wizard, 78-83
Add Printer Wizard dialog boxes, 79
Add Users and Groups dialog box, 102, 105, 108
Add/Remove Program Properties dialog box, 195
Administering a Windows NT network, 229-230
Administrator, defined, 66
Administrator privileges, 66
Appearances tab of Display Properties dialog box, 184
Application log (Event Viewer), 157
Application windows, 34, 36-38, 48
Applications. *See* Programs
Arranging program windows, 36-38, 48
Audit logs, 95, 110-112
Auditing command button, 111

B

Back Up program, 161-162
Background process, 24
BackOffice, 241-244
Batch file, explained, 150
Batch programs, explained, 249
Boot, explained, 7
Browsing the World Wide Web, 169-174
Buffer, defined, 152

C

Cabling, network, 226-228
Calculator, 21, 118-123
    moving values to and from, 121
    in scientific view, 121-123
Check boxes, 41
Close button, 24-25, 38
Closing windows, 38
Coaxial cabling, 227
Color scheme (desktop), changing, 183-185
Combo boxes, 43
Command prompt (MS-DOS), 149-154, 248
Commands (menu), 38-45
Commands (MS-DOS), table of, 248-251
Complexity of Windows NT, 10-11
Compression, disk, 213-215
Computers on a network, finding, 234-236
Console window
    control menu, 151
    copying and pasting to/from, 151
    customizing, 152-154

Console Window Properties dialog box, 153-154
Contents tab (Help window), 48-49
Control Panel folder, 149
Control Panel's Display tool, 43
Copy, defined, 63
Copying files, 62-63, 145
Copying and pasting to/from the console
    window, 151
Cost of Windows NT, 10
Crashes (program), explained, 8
Customizing Explorer and My Computer,
    190-194
Customizing menus, 187-194
Customizing the Start menu, 188-190
Customizing the task bar, 187-188
Customizing workstations, 177-202

D

Date (system)
        changing, 197-198
        displaying, 188
Date/Time Properties dialog box, 198
Default button, explained, 201
Deleting accounts, 98
Deleting files, 61, 144-145
Desktop shortcut icons, creating, 180-183
Desktop wallpaper, 186-187
Desktop (Windows NT), 19
        changing the background, 185-187
        changing the color scheme, 183-185
        changing the patterns on, 186
        redecorating, 183-187
Diagnostics program, 162
Dialog box common elements, 41-43
Dialog boxes, 40-45
Dial-Up Networking connection, 168
Disabling accounts, 98
Disconnect Network Drive dialog box, 148
Disconnecting network drives, 148
Disk Administrator program, 162
Disk compression, 213-215
Disk contents, viewing, 58-60, 142
Disk management, 63-66
Disk Properties dialog box, 213
Disk sharing, 66
Disk space, monitoring, 64-65, 146
Disk space issues, 221
Disks (floppy), formatting, 63-64, 146
Display Properties dialog box, 44
        Appearances tab, 184
        Settings tab, 45

Display tool (Control Panel), 43
Document files, 56
Document menu, clearing, 190
Document menu commands, 84-85
Document Properties dialog box, 85
Document windows, explained, 34
Documents
        definition of, 22
        opening, 22-23
        printing, 82-83
Domain controller, explained, 94, 228
Domains, explained, 94
DOS command prompt, 149-154, 248
DOS commands, table of, 248-251
Downloading files from the Web, 173-174
Drag, defined, 35
Driver, defined, 11
Drives (network)
        disconnecting, 148
        mapping, 68-70, 147-148
        working with, 70
Dvorak keyboard, defined, 200

E

Edit Speed Dial dialog box (Phone Dialer), 130
Editing an account, 98
Editing documents in WordPad, 131-132
Editing images in Paint, 126-127
Ellipses (...) in menus, 40
Event Detail screen, 156
Event Log Settings dialog box, 160
Event logs, 154-159
        filtering, 160-161
        housekeeping, 159-160
        saving and opening, 159
Event Viewer, 154-161
Exchange Server 4.0, 243
Explorer, 139-149
        changing the view, 191-194
        customizing, 190-194
        program window, 140
        working with files and folders, 141-149

F

FAT disk, setting share permissions on, 103-106
FAT file system, 221-222
Favorite places on the Web, 172
File Auditing dialog box, 111-112
File compression, 213-215

File Exit, 25
File icons, explained, 58
File manipulation, 60-64
File Permissions dialog box, 107
File system, selecting, 221-222
Files. *See also* Documents; Programs
     copying and moving, 62-63
     deleting and undeleting, 61, 144-145
     downloading from the Web, 173-174
     in Explorer, 141-149
     finding, 236-239
     most recently used, 61
     opening, 60-61, 143
     renaming, 61-62, 145
Filter dialog box (Event Viewer), 160
Find All Files window, 236
Find command, 233-239
Find Computer window, 234, 235
Find Files window, 237
Find tab (Help window), 50
Finding computers on a network, 233-236
Finding files and folders, 236-239
Fine-tuning Windows NT, 205-216
Floppy disks, formatting, 63-64, 146
Folder icons, explained, 58
Folders
     compressing, 213-215
     copying and moving files between, 62-63
     creating, 142
     explained, 59
     in Explorer, 141-149
     finding, 236-239
     renaming, 61-62, 145
     working with, 70
Foreground process, 23-24
Foreground program window, defined, 216
Format Disk dialog box, 64
Formatting floppy disks, 63-64, 146

G

Games, Windows NT, 39
Graphics images on a Web page, saving, 173
Groups (account), 95
     creating, 98-99
     editing, 99-100
     working with, 96-101

H

Hardware compatibility issues, 11, 221

Help, 47-50
Help Contents, 48-49
Help Index, 50
Help program window, 48, 49
Hide button, 37
Hiding windows, 37
Home page (World Wide Web), 169
Hyperlinks between Web pages, 169-171

I

Icons (shortcut). *See* Shortcut icons
Index tab (Help window), 50
Installing a new program, 194-195
Installing printers, 77-82
Installing Windows NT Server, 228-229
Installing Windows NT Workstation, 219-223
Install/Uninstall tab, 195
Internet, 165-174
     browsing the World Wide Web, 169-174
     connecting to, 167-168
Internet Information Server 1.0, 243
Internet Jumpstart Kit, 167
Intranet, defined, 243

K

Keyboard keys, adjusting, 199-200
Keyboard Properties dialog box, 199

L

List box, 42
List Names From dialog box, 101
Local group, 99
Local Group Properties dialog box, 99
Local printer, adding, 77-81
Lock Workstation, 27
Locking your computer, 27
Logging off, 25-27
Logging on as a different user, 27
Logging on to Windows NT, 18-19

M

Map Network Drive dialog box, 69-70, 147
Map Network Drive tool, 68
Mapping network drives, 68-70, 147-148
Maximize button, 37
Member server, defined, 228, 243

Memory, and running programs, 23
Menu bar, 39, 40
Menu ellipses (...), 40
Menus, 38-45
    customizing, 187-194
    shortcut, 46-47
Microsoft Excel icon, 59
Microsoft Exchange Server 4.0, 243
Microsoft Internet Information Server 1.0, 243
Microsoft SNA Server 2.11, 244
Microsoft software, advantages of, 9
Microsoft SQL Server 6.5, 243
Microsoft Systems Management Server 1.1, 244
Microsoft Word for Windows 95
    icon, 59
    Print dialog box, 83
    program window, 35, 46
Monitoring disk space, 64-65, 146
Mouse, adjusting, 200-201
Move, defined, 63
Moving files, 62-63, 145
Moving windows, 37
MS-DOS command prompt, 149-154, 248
MS-DOS commands, 248-251
Multiple programs, running, 18, 23-24
Multitasking, 18, 23-24
My Computer, 56-63
    changing the view, 191-194
    customizing, 190-194
    file icon display, 59
    Options window View tab, 193
    program window, 57
    shortcut icon, 57
    starting, 57-58

N

Naming a printer, 80-81
Network administration, 229-230
Network cabling, 226-228
Network cards, 226, 228
Network drives
    disconnecting, 148
    mapping, 68-70, 147-148
    working with, 70
Network Neighborhood, 148
    icon, 67
    overview, 67-68
    window, 68-69
Network printer, adding, 81-82
Network protocols, 228

Networks
    administering, 229-230
    exploring, 67-70
    finding computers on, 234-236
    setting up, 225-230
New account, creating, 97-98
New Local Group dialog box, 99
New User dialog box, 97-98
Normal Properties dialog box Security tab, 106
NT. *See* Windows NT
NTFS disk, setting share permissions on, 106-108
NTFS file system, 221-222

O

Online help feature, 47-50
Open dialog box in Paint, 128
Open With dialog box in Explorer, 143
Opening documents to start programs, 22-23
Opening files, 60-61, 143
Operating systems
    explained, 3-4
    Windows NT, types of, 80
Option buttons, 42
Ownership command button, 111

P

PAGE UP/PAGE DN, 36
Paint accessory, 123-128
    editing images, 126-127
    saving and printing images, 127-128
Performance tab of Task Manager window, 212
Permissions, 70, 95
    setting on a printer, 108-110
    share, 103-108
    working with, 102-110
Permissions (share)
    setting on a FAT disk, 103-106
    setting on an NTFS disk, 106-108
Phone Dialer accessory, 128-130
Policies for accounts, setting, 100-101
Power user tools, 135-162
Print dialog box, 42, 83
Print queue, 77, 84
Printer emulation, 80
Printer icons, 60
Printer menu commands, 86
Printer permissions, setting, 108-110
Printer Permissions dialog box, 110
Printer Properties dialog box, 109

Printers
  installing, 77-82
  naming, 80-81
  working with, 83-86
Printers folder, 149
Printers window, 78, 84
Printing, 73-87
  a document, 82-83
  documents in WordPad, 132-133
  how Windows NT prints, 76-77
  images in Paint, 127-128
Privileges. *See* Rights
Process, explained, 23, 211
Process priorities, changing, 210-212
Processes tab of Task Manager window, 210
Program files, 56
Program Speed Dial dialog box (Phone Dialer), 129
Program windows
  arranging, 36-38, 48
  explained, 34
Programs
  adding/installing, 194-195
  finding which are running, 209
  managing, 209-210
  removing, 194-195
  running multiple, 23-24
  starting, 19-23
  stopping/terminating, 24-25, 210
Properties dialog boxes, 65
  document, 85
  printer, 109
  Security tab, 111
  Sharing tab, 66

Q

Question mark button, 83

R

RAS connection, 168
Recycle Bin, 61-62
Recycle Bin Properties dialog box, 144
Regional settings, changing, 195-197
Regional Settings Properties dialog box, 196
Removing a program, 194-195
Renaming files and folders, 61-62, 145
Resize box, window, 38
Resizing windows, 37-38
Resolution (monitor display), explained, 183
Resource use, reviewing, 212-213
Restore button, 37
Right-clicking an object, 47
Rights, 94-95, 101-102
Running multiple programs, 23-24, 209-210

S

Safety, Windows NT, 8
Save As dialog box, 127, 173
Saving documents in WordPad, 132-133
Saving images in Paint, 127-128
Scroll bars, 35-36
Security, Windows NT, 6-7, 89-112
Security dialog box, 27, 208
Security log (Event Viewer), 157-159
Security tab (Properties dialog box), 106, 111
Service pack, defined, 229
Settings tab (Display Properties dialog box), 45
Share permissions
  setting on a FAT disk, 103-106
  setting on an NTFS disk, 106-108
Shared printer, naming, 80-81
Sharing disks, 66
Sharing tab (Properties dialog box), 66
SHIFT-TAB, 43
Shortcut icons, 21-22
  adding to the Start menu, 189
  adding to submenus, 189-190
  arranging, 182-183
  creating for your desktop, 180-183
  deleting and renaming, 182
  explained, 22
  in My Computer window, 58-60
  removing from submenus, 190
Shortcut menus, 46-47
Shut Down Windows dialog box, 26
Slider buttons (sliders), 43-44
SNA Server 2.11, 244
Solitaire game, 39-41
Sound Properties dialog box, 202
Sounds, changing, 201-202
Speed of Windows NT, 5-6
Spool file, explained, 76
Spool file display, 85
Spool files, 84
SQL Server 6.5, 243
Start button, 20-21
Start menu, 20
  customizing, 188-190
  Programs tab, 189
Starting programs, 19-23, 57-58
Stopping programs, 24-25

Submenus
    adding shortcuts to, 189
    definition of, 20
Symmetric processing, explained, 6
System date
    changing, 197-198
    displaying, 188
System process priorities, changing, 210-212
System Properties dialog box, 215-216
System time, changing, 197-198
System tool, using, 215-216
Systems Management Server 1.1, 244

T

TAB, 43
Tabs, 43-45
Task bar
    customizing, 187-188
    defined, 48
Task bar button, 23
Task Manager, 208-213
Task Manager window
    Performance tab, 212
    Processes tab, 210
Taskbar Properties dialog box, 188-189
Technical support, 230
Terminating a program, 210
Text boxes, 43
32-bit operating system, 5
Time (system), changing, 197-198
Time Zone map, 198
Title bar, explained, 34, 37
Toolbars, 45-46
Turning off your computer, 26

U

Uncompressing a disk, 214-215
Undeleting files, 61, 144-145
User Manager, 96-102
User Manager program window, 96
User Rights Policy dialog box, 101-102
UTP cabling, 227

V

View, changing, 191-194

W

Wallpapering the desktop, 186-187
Web browser, defined, 167
Web pages
    favorite places, 172
    hyperlinks between, 169-171
    moving back and forward between,
        171-172
    saving content from, 172-174
    using forms on, 174
Window resize box, 38
Windows, 34-38
    closing, 38
    hiding, 37
    moving, 37
    resizing, 37-38
Windows NT
    advantages of, 4-9
    complexity of, 10-11
    cost of, 10
    desktop, 19
    disadvantages of, 9-11
    fine-tuning, 205-216
    games, 39
    hardware compatibility issues, 11
    how it prints, 76-77
    logging on, 18-19
    from Microsoft, 9
    safety, 8
    security, 6-7, 89-112
    sounds, 201-202
    speed of, 5-6
    types of, 4, 80
Windows NT accessories, 115-133
Windows NT Diagnostics program, 162
Windows NT Explorer. *See* Explorer
Windows NT Server, 4, 228, 229
Windows NT Workstation, 4, 219-223
Word for Windows 95
    icon, 59
    Print dialog box, 83
    program window, 35, 46
WordPad accessory, 130-133
    editing documents, 131-132
    program window, 131
    saving and printing documents, 132-133
Workstations, customizing, 177-202
World Wide Web browsing, 169-174

DIGITAL DESIGN
FOR THE
21ST CENTURY

You can count on Osborne/McGraw-Hill and its expert authors to bring you the inside scoop on digital design, production, and the best-selling graphics software.

Digital Images: A Practical Guide
by Adele Droblas Greenberg
and Seth Greenberg
$26.95 U.S.A., ISBN 0-07-882113-4

Scanning the Professional Way
by Sybil Ihrig and Emil Ihrig
$21.95 U.S.A., ISBN 0-07-882145-2

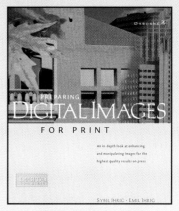

Preparing Digital Images for Print
by Sybil Ihrig and Emil Ihrig
$21.95 U.S.A., ISBN 0-07-882146-0

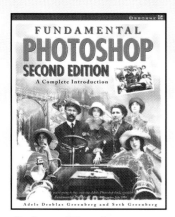

**Fundamental Photoshop:
A Complete Introduction,
Second Edition**
by Adele Droblas Greenberg and Seth Greenberg
$29.95 U.S.A., ISBN 0-07-882093-6

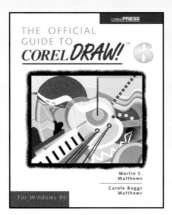

**The Official Guide to
CorelDRAW!™6 for Windows 95**
by Martin S. Matthews and Carole Boggs Matthews
$34.95 U.S.A., ISBN 0-07-882168-1

**The Official Guide to Corel
PHOTO-PAINT 6**
by David Huss
$34.95 U.S.A., ISBN 0-07-882207-6

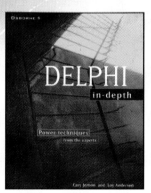

FUTURE CLASSICS FROM

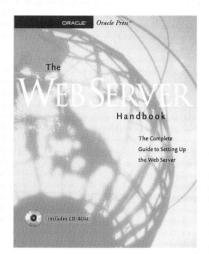

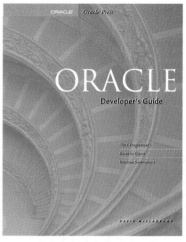

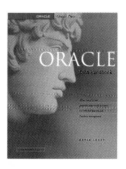

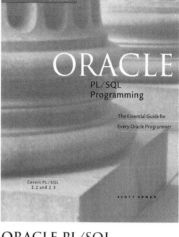
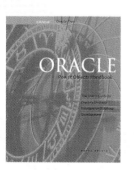

The Books to Use When There's

Save Time and Get

the Information You

Need with this Critically

Acclaimed Series from

Osborne/McGraw-Hill.

**The Internet
for Busy People**
by Christian Crumlish
$22.95 USA
ISBN: 0-07-882108-8

**Windows 95
for Busy People**
by Ron Mansfield
$22.95 USA
ISBN: 0-07-882110-X

**Word for Windows 95
for Busy People**
by Christian Crumlish
$22.95 USA
ISBN: 0-07-882109-6

**Excel for Windows 95
for Busy People**
by Ron Mansfield
$22.95 USA
ISBN: 0-07-882111-8

No Time to Lose!

Computer Fundamentals for Complicated Lives

Whether you set aside an evening or lunch hour, reach for a **BUSY PEOPLE** guide and you're guaranteed to save time! Organized for a quick orientation to the most popular computer hardware and software applications, each **BUSY PEOPLE** title offers exceptional timesaving features and has the right blend of vital skills and handy shortcuts that you must know to get a job done quickly and accurately. Full-color text makes the going easy and fun.

Written by a busy person (like you!) with a skeptic's view of computing, these opinionated, well-organized, and authoritative books are all you'll need to master the important ins and outs of the best-selling software releases, hardware, and the Internet—without wasting your precious hours!

Access for Windows 95 for Busy People
by Alan Neibauer
$22.95 USA
ISBN: 0-07-882112-6

PCs for Busy People
by David Einstein
$22.95 USA
ISBN: 0-07-882210-6

PowerPoint for Windows 95 for Busy People
by Ron Mansfield
$22.95 USA
ISBN: 0-07-882204-1

Web Publishing with Netscape for Busy People
by Christian Crumlish and Malcolm Humes
$22.95 USA
ISBN: 0-07-882144-4

http:// www.osborne.com

OSBORNE

ORDER BOOKS DIRECTLY FROM OSBORNE/McGRAW-HILL

For a complete catalog of Osborne's books, call 510-549-6600 or write to us at 2600 Tenth Street, Berkeley, CA 94710

Call Toll-Free, *24 hours a day, 7 days a week, in the U.S.A.*
U.S.A.: 1-800-262-4729   **Canada: 1-800-565-5758**

Mail *in the U.S.A. to:*   **Canada**
McGraw-Hill, Inc.   *McGraw-Hill Ryerson*
Customer Service Dept.   *Customer Service*
P.O. Box 182607   *300 Water Street*
Columbus, OH 43218-2607   *Whitby, Ontario L1N 9B6*

Fax *in the U.S.A. to:*   **Canada**
1-614-759-3644   **1-800-463-5885**
                                          Canada
                                          orders@mcgrawhill.ca

SHIP TO:

Name _____

Company _____

Address _____

City / State / Zip _____

Daytime Telephone *(We'll contact you if there's a question about your order.)*

ISBN #	BOOK TITLE	Quantity	Price	Total
0-07-88				
0-07-88				
0-07-88				
0-07-88				
0-07-88				
0-07088				
0-07-88				
0-07-88				
0-07-88				
0-07-88				
0-07-88				
0-07-88				
0-07-88				
0-07-88				

Shipping & Handling Charge from Chart Below

Subtotal

Please Add Applicable State & Local Sales Tax

TOTAL

Shipping & Handling Charges

Order Amount	U.S.	Outside U.S.
$15.00 - $24.99	$4.00	$6.00
$25.00 - $49.99	$5.00	$7.00
$50.00 - $74.99	$6.00	$8.00
$75.00 - and up	$7.00	$9.00
$100.00 - and up	$8.00	$10.00

Occasionally we allow other selected companies to use our mailing list. If you would prefer that we not include you in these extra mailings, please check here: ❏

METHOD OF PAYMENT

❏ Check or money order enclosed (payable to Osborne/McGraw-Hill)

❏ AMERICAN EXPRESS   ❏ DISCOVER   ❏ MasterCard.   ❏ VISA

Account No. [ ][ ][ ][ ][ ][ ][ ][ ][ ][ ][ ][ ][ ][ ][ ][ ]

Expiration Date _____

Signature _____

In a hurry? Call with your order anytime, day or night, or visit your local bookstore.

Thank you for your order   Code BC640SL